Mainstay Press publishes books geared to social change. Mainstay books illuminate the realities and possibilities of contemporary social and political life – the life of the public that profoundly involves the personal lives of people everywhere.

WESTERN TERROR

FROM POTOSÍ TO BAGHDAD

Andre Vltchek

Mainstay Press

Mainstay Press

Copyright © 2006 by Andre Vltchek

Cover photo by Andre Vltchek

ISBN: 0-9774590-3-9

Mainstay is funded in part by the Puffin Foundation

Preface	9
Western Terror: From Potosi to Baghdad	17
Aid For The Rich	31
New Violence In Gujarat 　Don't Blame It Just On Muslims	37
The War Against Latin American Poor	47
North Korea: Who's Afraid Of Whom	63
Amnesia In Rhodes	69
Self Censorship In The US 　Not Unlike The Soviet Version	77
Asia And The War With Iraq	85
The New, Deadly Beginning Of History	95
Cowardly War	101
Castro's Loneliness in Asia	109
War Against The War 　by Andre Vltchek and William Toth	117
"Activist Nuns" From Tennessee 　by Andre Vltchek and William Toth	125
Malaysia and Singapore Revisited	133
East Timor – Indonesian Amnesia	145

So Where Was the Resistance?	153
Indonesia – Not Even Yet At The Crossroad	161
Alberto Fujimori And Japanese Racism	173
Thailand: What's Going On?	181
East Timor – Australia's Shame	187
Will Indonesia Be Saved By "Euro – 2004"?	195
Is It Wrong To Defend Najaf?	201
Defending Venezuela	207
Indonesia Teaching France About Freedom?	213
Are We Alone, Arundhati Roy?	221
Republicans Won, The Rest Of The World Lost	231
Aceh Goes To Heaven!	239
Aceh Abandoned – The Second Tsunami	249
Bitter Victory Of Blair	269
Colonia Dignidad In Chile – Fall Of The "gods"	275
Hurricane Katrina – View From Asia	283
Coming Back Home – To New York	291

Preface

Ever since I was a very young man, I have been traveling all over the world, living in different countries, learning new languages, searching for good stories; political and personal. As time passed I was able to shed all racial and cultural preferences, accepting the world as it is – rich and exciting in its diversity.

My work as a journalist and war correspondent took me to some far away (from the Western perspective) places: from East Timor and Papua to the Peruvian Andes, from Sri Lanka and Gujarat to Chiapas, from the frozen plains of Siberia to the hot, burning metal shacks of the Soweto Township near Johannesburg. I wrote fiction and poetry, but I also worked for some media giants like Asahi Shimbun in Tokyo, MFD in Prague, ABC News in the United States, even Hurriyet in Istanbul. And I also wrote for emerging publications in the Czech Republic, Peru, Indonesia, Nepal and many other places.

What I learned at a fairly young age was that almost no major media wanted me to cover the "real world"; its complexity, its problems that go back to the period of colonialism. Nobody allowed me to write about the almost total Western economic, political and cultural control over the world. I tried to resist, to file good and honest stories from "controversial" places. Most of them were outright rejected or trimmed beyond recognition.

"Colonia Dignidad – never again!" I was told by the US based editor of the influential German magazine Der Stern, after offering him complete new evidence on the brutality of a German – Nazi camp in Southern Chile. All my stories about the insane Indonesian military's genocidal actions in Ermera and other regions of East Timor were never even considered – Suharto and his generals were western allies, benevolent authoritarian figures, our good lackeys.

Technology had been changing; from slowly crawling faxes to mobile phones, followed by satellite phones and digital cameras. Transmission of information and images became fast and reliable, but messages were increasingly shallow, unchallenging, lacking historical, cultural and philosophical insights. Despite the speed of transmission, people all over the world were being put on an unappetizing diet of half-truths and shallow simplifications, often of outright lies. Consumers of the dominant news channels and newspapers worldwide – all fed from similar sources – were becoming increasingly indifferent, and almost phlegmatic.

Hunger, war and despair were no longer shocking anybody. To worry about billions of people all over the world living in a gutter would gain one a label of "extremist," "radical," basically an outcast.

The plunder continued. The center of power of world order with its seeds in past centuries of colonial plunder moved to nontransparent boardrooms of multinational companies. Elected governments were now serving business interests much more than the interests of those who voted for them. Elections were becoming increasingly irrelevant as the mass media owned by the new masters of the universe decided which ideas and which political parties to promote. The fabled "balance of power" in the United States collapsed like a house of cards: one additional, unelected and unbalanced power – big business – was now able to keep in check the entire system painstakingly designed by the Founding Fathers.

The United Nations collapsed as well, becoming not much more than another humiliated and powerless museum piece of some of the greatest aspirations of humanity. Its attempted rebuffs of neo-colonial states were met by financial blackmail and threats to make it irrelevant – something that had already happened many years earlier. Considering that the United Nations is nothing other than an organization representing almost all nations of the world, what was actually made irrelevant was the will of the great majority of the countries on this planet.

I saw it all from both sides: from rich North America, Japan, Singapore and Europe – and also from desperate Honduras and Nicaragua, Swaziland and Bangladesh, Papua and East Timor.

I often fantasized about what would happen if our planet were visited by a spaceship from another galaxy inhabited by much more developed and intelligent creatures that are truly cherishing equality and compassion, dignity as well as justice for all. What if they would circle the earth and listen to the speeches of our politicians and corporate heads, while watching through giant telescopes real life on the surface of our planet? My conclusion was that they would puke.

I myself could not stomach it anymore. I left the mainstream, began writing books and articles for independent media, and launched my own web-based magazine WCN[1]. I put together a good team of international journalists from every corner of the world, but soon realized that globalization served only those who were really big, not enthusiastic writers and reporters like us. While I was in some ways "globalized" as well (living all over the world, refusing to belong anywhere), I had been shown that I misunderstood the rules of the game: globalization was for the companies, it was for "goods and services," for business – not for the members of the opposition. WCN – with no geographical base, with no permanent mailing address and no bank willing to allow it to process credit card subscriptions – eventually went into hibernation.

I became a senior fellow at the Oakland Institute[2], a progressive political think-tank. A few months later I received an email from two great writers, Tony Christini and Mike Palecek, inviting me to become a cofounder of the new publishing house which would promote political fiction and

---

[1] www.worldconfrontationnow.com

[2] www.oaklandinstitute.org

some nonfiction. A few months later, Mainstay Press[3] was born.

I never believed that I was born to be a rebel, a dissident, although it became obvious that no matter where I lived I ended up in dissent. Then I felt that I had no choice but to become one, as I felt no desire to become just another helpless bystander. As a kid growing up in Central Europe I was taught that not helping a person who is bleeding or hurt in the middle of the road is a crime. Let's now apply this very correct logic to the global arrangement.

Not only do most of us – fortunate ones – do nothing to help, we pretend that nothing monstrous is taking place. While hundreds of millions are dying from malnutrition and curable diseases, we go to sleep with clear a conscience, satisfied that our governments and corporate leaders have pledged a few million dollars to tackle the problem. While our missiles with depleted uranium are bashing some miserable towns thousands of miles away, we say to ourselves that our invasion will lessen suffering over the long term. When our companies exploit desperate people in developing countries, we reply that we are helping to create jobs. And when our establishment supports some bloody coup against some progressive and democratically elected government, we pretend that we don't know; we forget how to read between the lines. Not all of us, but many; still the majority.

Our indifference is finishing Africa – a continent plundered by poverty and disease which the West divided and exploited for centuries; and Latin America – first robbed of its gods and languages, enslaved and now finally resisting our total

---
[3] www.mainstaypress.org

political and economic domination; and the Middle East – our open playground where we overthrew progressive and secular governments, supported some of the most heinous dictators, gassed people and exploited natural resources, offering to help with the unyielding determination of the Israeli right-wing to continue the colonization of the West Bank and Gaza; and the Pacific island nations and Southeast Asia – our tremendous orgy of terror against civilian populations from Vietnam to Laos and Cambodia, to support of Suharto's military coup in 1965 that destroyed the nation and killed millions of innocent people and later led to the invasion of East Timor and one of the worst genocides in the history of mankind.

A writer who refuses to tell the truth is a liar. A writer who refuses to lie in these dark days is an outcast. To my surprise, despite being labeled as "opposition" or "dissident," I saw my articles being reprinted and translated into several languages world-wide, mainly thanks to the outlet for many of the following commentaries – "Z-Magazine/Z-Net."

The articles and commentaries which form this volume appeared in different publications and sites and were written during the last 4 years, after September 11 and during the invasion of Afghanistan and Iraq, the reelection of Bush and Blair, the devastating tsunami in Aceh and a shameful response to hurricane Katrina.

I see this book as my private tribute to those men and women worldwide who refused to accept indoctrination and who continue to search for the truth. I see this book also a tribute to those brave human beings who suffered but resisted our political terror in jails and torture chambers in Chile and Argentina, in Salvador and Guatemala, in the Buru concentration camp in Indonesia, everywhere we have supported inhuman regimes in order to serve our business and geo-political interests.

Jakarta, January 2006

Andre Vltchek

Western Terror: From Potosí to Baghdad

The North American empire is admired by some, condemned by others, but feared by all. There are those, including the British prime minister, who sees it as the mighty defender of the civilized world's values. For many people, it is the world's most potent terrorist state – mostly those who have tasted the brutality of U.S. foreign policy in dozens of unfortunate places all over the world.

But is the responsibility for the pitiful state of today's world exclusively American? Is the United States unique in its ruthlessness, after all? Is there anything new and creative in its post-colonial, arrogant, and thuggish approach toward the world?

The answer to both questions is "No."

There is nothing original in the desire of the U.S. to impose its western economic and cultural will upon the rest of the planet. For centuries, the world had been terrorized and plundered by numerous European powers.

Disregard for the interests of people with different skin color, cultures, philosophies, religions, languages, ways of life, and socio-economic structures is not something recently invented in Washington DC or New York City. All European empires built their fortunes by plundering the world. Silver from the mines of Potosí, spices from the Indonesian archipelago, precious stones and even trade in human beings from Africa, all paying for gigantic palaces, museums and theaters, for cathedrals and municipal buildings – for almost everything that we now call "western civilization."

Not unlike the present day, the rest of the world always had a free choice, "be with us or be against us." To be "with us" meant (and still means) "to serve us."

We must never forget that the West behaved as if it had an inherited, but undefined, right to profit from the misery of the rest of the world. In many cases, the conquered nations (for many cases, read most of the nations of the world) had to give up their own culture, their religions, even their languages, and convert to our set of beliefs and values that we defined as "civilized." The West has never doubted that its cause is the only one that is just, its religions the only ones that lead to God, its greed (whether it is called capitalism or the market economy) the only pure and honest expression of human nature.

During the colonial era, Europe acted like a brutal thug. In comparison to its colonial armies, any present-day terrorist group looks like nothing more than a bunch of second-graders. Colonial powers (past and present) vigorously imposed religious, racial, and other dogmas. No opposition was tolerated. Any kind of expression of dissent, especially that coming from men and women of enslaved nations, was brutally suppressed.

European terror and greed has, for centuries, plundered the great civilizations of Africa, Central and South America, the Middle East, and Asia. No official apology has ever been issued; no compensation has ever been paid. The topic is taboo, even though the plunder continues in a post-colonial manner, utilizing so-called globalization, and the increasing power of unaccountable multinational companies. Most left-wing European intellectuals conveniently place the burden of responsibility exclusively on the shoulders of the United States, its government, and its companies. Shockingly, Europe, by cashing in on its few half-hearted critics of U.S. foreign policy, somehow manages to feel morally superior.

The same is happening in South America. While the U.S. terror against sovereign Latin nations and their progressive governments and movements in the 20th century is well remembered, the terror of the Spanish conquest seems to have been forgotten and forgiven, at least by the ruling whites, regardless of their position (on the right or the left) in the political spectrum.

It is unnecessary to say that the Latin American system of power is one of the most cynical examples of European colonial legacy: most of the continent is still ruled by the European minority, while indigenous populations are discriminated against by ruling elites that feel closer to the West than to their own countries. Brazil, for instance, has the fourth-worst disparity of income distribution in the world, and Chile (often hailed as an economic star performer) is not far behind.

U.S. bashing is very much the vogue in cafes of Santiago de Chile. It would be just and appropriate if the U.S. were to be criticized for its countless crimes, such as the orchestration of the coup against Salvador Allende on September 11, 1973 or its support for the abortive coup against Hugo Chavez earlier this year. But Allende is now looked down upon by most Chileans, the result of long decades of a successful brainwashing campaign. Chavez is no longer celebrated as a great reformist, friend of the poor, and the only truly brave and democratic South American leader. Almost everyone in Chile, including those who call themselves leftists, have accepted right-wing propaganda that labels Chavez as a populist demagogue and would-be tyrant.

South American intellectual hostility toward the U.S., and its supine admiration of everything European, is often based more on unsatisfied desire and suffers from the European cultural superiority complex rather than any real opposition to U.S. foreign policy. Many intellectuals in South America are of European stock, holding at least one European passport (granted because of their "blood") and desperately need to demonstrate their European identity to themselves, and to the whole world. Many of these pseudo-leftists are not really against the U.S., they are against everything American in general, good and bad, from Big Macs to original cultures of the South American continent and its indigenous people.

Without mentioning European plunder, rape, and murder in Central and South America, without speaking of racist European-descent rulers who are still in control of the majority of Latin American countries and their economies, singling out U.S. policy toward Latin America as solely responsible for the current situation would be out of context.

It is worth noting that many Latin intellectuals who are always ready to ridicule "big brother in the North" as the exclusive culprit, are simultaneously hostile to any serious opposition to the new world order. Their worst nightmares, it seems, are about people like Venezuelan President Hugo Chavez, who dares to address the grievances of the poor world that is not particularly white.

U.S. foreign policy toward Latin America has been reprehensible for decades and centuries. It can justly be described in one word – terrorism. But again, the U.S. is not the one that invented the wheel, nor is it the only one that sits in the driver's seat. Even its worst excesses have not managed to exterminate 20, 50 or, as was the case during the French invasion of Grenada in the 17th century, even 100 percent of the population of the territories of its modern day colonies.

Eduardo Galeano wrote in his "Open Veins of Latin America," "Spain owned the cow, while Europe drank the milk."

Geopolitics have changed. The U.S. and its companies now own many cows, including those in Latin America. But do you hear that contented sucking sound coming from Europe and the Far East? While Japan is often justifiably attacked for its stubborn refusal to apologize openly to Korea and the other countries that it occupied before and after the Second World War, Europe still treasures its shameful colonial past. If it were only the past, let it be – but European world rule gave birth to the present global power structure and provided the foundation for today's world order, for American imperialism, and for one-way cultural globalization.

Remarkably, European justifications have existed virtually unchallenged until recently. Hardly anyone in Europe or in the United States spends sleepless nights wondering why four out of the five countries that belong to the UN Security Council – the UK, France, Russia, and the U.S. – are former and, to some extent, present colonial powers with absolutely no moral mandate to advise the world on what is right and wrong.

While preparing to invade Iraq because of some unconfirmed speculations that it has weapons of mass destruction, the world is supposed to feel comfortable knowing that several western powers like UK, France, Russia, and the U.S. are sitting on enormous arsenals of such weapons and proudly noting it. In the distant, and not so distant, past, all four nations terrorized dozens of countries and regions all over the world. Who gave them a mandate to be sole masters of the universe?

The answer is, of course, "nobody." But, somehow, everything is justified by a blurry dogma and popular belief in the West, perfected during several centuries of European colonial rule. The finished product was a conviction that defining "civilization" and, above all, deciding what is "right" and "wrong," should take place in European capitals and, lately, in Washington, instead of anywhere else in the world.

Should those butchered by the French, the British, the Americans, and the Russians reserve the right of a pre-emptive strike based on their justifiable fear and concern that what had been done to them once might be done again? That would be unthinkable. That would be defined as "terrorism."

It's only us, only the West, that can make decisions on such important matters.

At present, geopolitically irrelevant countries, such as the UK, Russia, and France (is there anything that makes them more important than much bigger non-western nations, except a determined belief in their cultural and racial superiority?), representing nobody but themselves, are on the Security Council making sure that their voices are heard. Other enormous nations and geographical and cultural blocks, are not allowed to participate in world decision-making. Why has France, with about sixty million people, the right to veto UN resolutions, while India, with over one billion, has not? Why is the British vote more powerful than those of all Latin America and Africa combined?

Considering this, can we really talk of a U.S.-dominated world, or should we admit that a fraternity of western countries rules the world, as it has done for centuries?

It is a fraternity that rules the rest of the world by virtue of its control of the UN Security Council and the world economy and culture. It controls linguistics by polluting the languages of the world with terms such as freedom, democracy, and liberty, words that have lost their meaning, but are still supposed to define western superiority, as well as by many other means. It is a fraternity with its cultural, political, and imperialistic roots firmly planted in all parts of the body of the old continent.

In the recent past, Spain celebrated the 500th anniversary of the discovery of the "New World" – in reality the beginning of one of the most perverted and sadistic chapters in the history of humanity. During the Spanish conquest, the colonized nations were given the choice referred to earlier: be with us (become our slaves and bury your culture and free will forever) or be against us (be tortured to death or exterminated).

The French still cling to their idea of a Francophone world – for that, read "the part of the world where the French language was pushed down the throat of the colonized people."

Writing these words in Hanoi, from my window I can see a corner of the central jail, now a national monument of Vietnam, that commemorates the victims of brutal torture and executions performed by French colonizers on the local people. As in so many other places colonized by European powers, the inhabitants of Indochina were stripped of their dignity, robbed, and enslaved. It seems that everyone in the world recalls the dreadful brutality of the U.S. armed forces in Vietnam, but hardly anyone wants to remember French terror in Indochina. The only ones who seem to remember are the Vietnamese and the other inhabitants of Indochina's nations. Of course, nobody speaks French in Vietnam anymore, apart from a few very old men and women. The naiveté of the French would be almost touching, if it wasn't so monstrous: how can a nation torture, kill, and steal from another nation for decades, then return and wonder why almost no one wants to learn their language.

Half-hearted criticism of the present U.S. foreign policy by European intellectuals will not lift the burden of the responsibility that the old continent should feel for the present state of the world. For centuries, the world had been assaulted by European greed, enriching one small continent at the expense of the rest of the planet. After the Second

World War, the U.S. surpassed Europe as the prime world ruler; while improvement is not always visible, there should be little or no doubt that the situation would be much worse if Europe had retained its control over the world.

Consider the tens of millions of victims in Central and South America, the Caribbean, Africa, the Middle East and Asia; massacres of native people in North America and Australia, mostly performed by the first and second generation of European immigrants, the 100 Years War, the 30 Years War, the First World War, the Holocaust and the Second World War. This is only a short summary of the dark side of the glorified western civilization under European leadership. In the 20th century alone, over 100 million men, women and children were murdered in the wars, conflicts and the Holocaust.

Noam Chomsky calls the U.S. "an offspring of Europe." Despite its claim to be culturally diverse, the United States is based almost exclusively on western/Christian values. President George W. Bush is a Christian fundamentalist, not a Muslim or Buddhist scholar. The U.S. Senate still looks like an exclusive, rich, white boys club. One wonders; how many congresspeople were influenced by Confucian philosophers, how many of them ever studied Shinto or Islam? How many Supreme Court justices ever learned languages such as Thai, Swahili, Quechua or Mandarin?

All members of the loosely defined club of the rich nations (call it the OECD or anything you choose, but it generally consists of the U.S. and Canada, western and central Europe, Japan, Singapore, Hong Kong, Australia, and New Zealand), have more or less identical global interests. Criticism of U.S. foreign policy by its allies, if it occurs at all, is half-hearted and serves mostly short-term domestic interests, as in the recent 2002 elections in Germany, for instance.

The United States acts in the interest of the members of the club of the rich and against those of the majority of the world that remains poor and is mainly controlled by "bandit" governments friendly to the business interests of the rich world. It therefore enjoys the wholehearted support of the political and economic establishment in Europe and several rich countries in Asia.

While the U.S. prefers to play its role openly, other ruling states are much more discreet. The U.S. invasion of Iraq, the so-called Gulf War, was funded by Japan and Germany, countries that preferred to shed cash instead of sending combatants.

Of course, in order to create some sort of vision of global democracy and political and intellectual diversity, various European governments express disagreement with U.S. foreign policy from time to time. Such altercations typically last no more than several days or weeks before the U.S. is again promised support and eternal friendship.

No matter how brutal the U.S. aggression – whether in Vietnam, Laos, Cambodia, Grenada or indirectly in El Salvador[4], Guatemala, Chile, Nicaragua and elsewhere – no European or rich Asian country – nor any other member of the rich part of the world – ever came to the rescue of the

---

[4] Although, as the *Washington Post* notes, "U.S. authorities now acknowledge" that at least 21 U.S. troops were killed in action in El Salvador and that there are "more than 5,000 U.S. veterans of El Salvador's civil war." U.S. personnel are also known to have engaged directly in state terrorism in Guatemala and Nicaragua and elsewhere.

innocent victims. Even the very rare diplomatic condemnations of U.S. acts of terror were extremely vague.

The rich world has common interests, and pursues them consistently and ruthlessly. The poor world that makes up the overwhelming majority of our planet, has common interests as well, but is effectively prevented from defending them. The United States does the shooting, and the rest of its allies carry, reload and hold the gun. Call it "partnership," "cooperation," or whatever word you choose – the outcome is the same: the world dictatorship is enforced by one group, not by one country.

The U.S. is not the only country responsible for the present day global dictatorship. However, it is the most visible one. It does most of the shouting and shooting. It often wears ugly military fatigues. It has incredibly bad speech writers and government members like Rumsfeld, a man who looks like he could do some very ugly things with one's body and brain if allowed. The U.S. is still too much in love with itself, too willing to brag about its power to the rest of the world.

Europe is old and much more cynical. It knows the game. It doesn't offer too many words, doesn't send too many soldiers unnecessarily. While the young friend across the Atlantic does all the yelling and bombing voluntarily, it concentrates on its favorite activity of making and saving money.

But, don't be fooled. If threatened, if its power were to be challenged, if its position in the world was ever put in doubt, the old continent would become active again to defend what it believes is its right to maintain its privileged position.

The world is being increasingly divided into the rich and poor, into the powerful and powerless, into those who suffer and those who make others suffer. Responsibility for this morally contemptible situation lies equally at the doorsteps of the old and the new world. The most brutal chapter of human greed and terror probably started during the conquest of what is now Mexico. Or maybe it started in the corridors of devilishly cold silver mines, high in the Andes, in Potosí. Or maybe much earlier. It continues until now. Before the Spanish conquest, the Inca Empire was not perfect. Of course, no human society can be. Iraq under Saddam Hussein is very far from perfection, too. But we had no right then, and we do not have the right now, to enter foreign lands, to kill men and women, to change their rulers, to impose our interests.

After long decades and centuries of cooperation between the old and the new colonial powers, Europe had a unique chance to prove that it is different, that it has changed, that it repents its past and is willing to come to the defense of those who are defenseless. If it would say "No" to the U.S. war plans instead of using vague diplomatic language that no one can figure out, there could be some hope for pluralism, for a world that is not dominated by a single ideology and just one set of interests.

But Europe went along with the attack on Iraq; it stood on the sidelines as it did in Indochina and Central America during the reign of U.S. terror and it will have to bear the same moral responsibility as its offspring, the United States.

November 2002

Aid For The Rich

While the number of casualties from devastating floods are mounting in India, Nepal, Bangladesh and China, the rich part of the world averts its eyes, concentrating on the Czech Republic, Germany and Austria. In Prague, flood water filled several stations of the subway system in the ancient city of Prague, while threatening historic landmarks like the Charles Bridge and National Opera. Water from Vltava River irreversibly damaged some parts of what is repeatedly called by BBC World a jewel of Central Europe.

Just across the border, one of the German cultural capitals – Dresden – had to mobilize thousands of emergency workers and volunteers in order to save famous architectural landmarks like Zwinger palace and Semper Opera House.

Almost one hundred people have died in floods in the Czech Republic, Austria, Germany, Russia and Romania.

Without delay, the US and Scandinavian countries shifted to Prague heavy pumping equipment while the White House pledged generous financial aid. The European Union (which Czechs will probably join in 2004) has promised $63 million in relief. EU Commission President Romano Prodi embarked on a journey to Prague in order to meet President Vaclav Havel to assess the situation and offer further support to this richest country of the former Soviet block (a member of NATO, with the GDP per capita of $13,990 calculated on the PPP basis). President Bush called Czech President Vaclav Havel, promising, "The United States would rush supplies and monetary assistance to the Czech Republic to help areas devastated by flooding." Next door, the German government announced hundreds of millions of euros in relief for German flood victims.

All the international news channels (including BBC World, Deutche Welle and CNN International) are continuously offering in-depth live coverage of the tragedy to viewers all over the world.

While the world continues to mourn for European palaces, cathedrals, museums and flood victims, devastating floods and landslides have swept through China's southern provinces, killing at least 133 people. In neighboring Viet Nam, at least 10 people died during the past week.

Millions have been displaced in Bangladesh, India and Nepal – a part of the world that has continued to suffer from the annual monsoon floods since June. By now the death toll from floods has reached 911 in South Asia, displacing or trapping 25 million of mostly poor people. Nepal has suffered the heaviest losses with 424 people losing their lives.

On the other side of the globe, 10 people died in central Mexico, where heavy rains burst two dams, including one near San Luis Potosí, burying several villages under water.

Information about the ongoing tragedies in South Asia, China and Mexico hardly appear on the television screens of the wealthy countries. Cables coming from Asia and Latin America carry no words such as "aid" or "relief." No promises are being made to the people from these "far away places" who are obviously suffering from global warming effects mainly triggered by the rich world and its unbridled consumption. No heavy equipment is being shifted to India, Nepal, Bangladesh or China from US Navy bases or from the compassionate Scandinavian countries.

As always, the rich world is ready to defend its citizens, totally neglecting the plight of the poor in other parts of the world. The destruction of cozy houses in the Bavarian city of Passau easily evokes more concern in the West than the displacement of millions of poor peasants in India. The flooded cellars of Prague's National Theatre mobilize far more assistance than the destruction of Mexican villages.

Human life has a different value, depending on where it is being threatened, and it doesn't take 9-11 to realize it. This sad fact is unfortunately accepted even by some of the poorest countries themselves. Viet Nam News, The National English Newspaper, carries long articles about the flood situation in Europe, hardly mentioning that some poor neighborhoods of Hanoi on the banks of the Red River are currently under water.

In Nepal, The Red Cross is appealing for $1.6 million to help provide food, shelter, blankets, clothing and water purification tablets to flood victims. This is truly a pittance, if one considers the magnitude of the tragedy. The indirect message from the rich world is that the poor countries should be grateful for anything, even if the amount is almost insulting. Forget about the $63 million that rich Prague has been promised by the EU in the first stage of relief.

Compassion for the poor victims of natural disasters is usually not in the dictionary of rich countries. While the International Red Cross sought to raise $7.4 million in emergency aid for Central American countries devastated by Hurricane Mitch (1998), these very same countries were paying $2.2 million every day in debt service to their creditors. When begged to cancel the debt, The World Bank responded, "Although there is a great deal of sympathy for the devastated countries, it would be unfair, impossible and ultimately irresponsible to end the debt burden and walk away." No substantial help for the hurricane victims was ever delivered. Years later, hundreds of thousands of people in Nicaragua and Honduras are, once again, on the verge of starvation.

Czech, German and Austrian emergency units and armed forces are already cleaning the mess left by the flooding. Insurance companies are opening their wallets, governments are talking about emergency relief funds, newspapers (including Lidove noviny in Prague) are advising their readers on how to file claims to get the maximum amount of money from insurers and the government. Sympathy and funds are literally pouring into Central Europe. The long list of threatened "architectural jewels" is mentioned over and over again in thousands of detailed reports. Czech and German emergency shelters are providing victims with much food, medical care and above all, limitless sympathy.

In the meantime, the poor in South Asia, Mexico and China are holding tight to the little bundles they were able to rescue from their flooded homes and shacks, living in miserable conditions, mostly with no access to clean water or medicine. Most of them are uncertain about their immediate future. One wonders if any of the poor realizes that in today's world one has to be white and rich in order to evoke compassion and receive support and aid when disaster strikes.

August 2002

New Violence In Gujarat

Don't Blame It Just On Muslims

The night was dark, but the enormous Akshardham Temple and the Cultural Complex in Gandhinagar, belonging to the powerful Swaminarayam sect of Hinduism, was brightly illuminated. Sounds of sporadic explosions and gunfire were coming from the direction of the temple, while the crowd behind the main gate roared, trying to push through the security cordon to get closer to the fighting. Ambulances, police and military trucks were moving in. Two bungalows, formerly a visitor center, had been transformed into an emergency medical facility and a gathering place for local politicians.

Gujarat, a western Indian state known for its religious intolerance and violence, was living yet another nightmare. On September 24th, an unidentified number of gunmen entered the premises of the sect, closely linked to the RSS and the Indian ruling Party, BJP, and began spraying the 600 or so worshippers and visitors packed into main hall with bullets and hand grenades. Several people died on the spot, others barricaded themselves in one of the rooms of the temple, behind a heavy door. Police officers moved in few minutes later, but were unable to disarm the militants. The standoff lasted until the following day.

"The Indian government should attack the terrorists' training camps," declared Dr. Jaideep Patel, VHP (World Hindu Council), one of the chief organizers of the February anti-Muslim riots in Gujarat that left almost 1,500 people, mainly Muslims, dead. "Yes, the attackers are Muslim jihadis and this was a pre-planned attack."

A few feet away, another VHP member, Prakash C. Sevkani, was recalling nostalgically how he distributed swords during the riot. "Now the situation could explode at any moment. There is plenty of tension."

The Home Minister of Gujarat, Gardhan Zadaphia, refused to negotiate with the militants. "They are holding no hostages and there is no way we will compromise. We'll finish them off: we'll fight them until they are dead."

Before elite commandos arrived from the capital Delhi, badly armed and badly trained police officers were trying, unsuccessfully, to liquidate the intruders. Several members of the police force were injured by shrapnel and evacuated to the hospital, amid loud cheers from the crowd. At that point, officials spoke of some four or five attackers inside the compound.

On the next morning, the elite troops, the 'Black Cats', stormed the temple and killed the militants. There were only two of them. Officials claimed that one of them had been carrying a letter in his pocket, written by a previously unknown group called Tehriq-e-Qasas (Movement For Revenge). This letter was written in Urdu, a language used by both Indian Muslims and Pakistanis. The source of the English translation is unknown: it appears here in unedited form:

> Movement For Revenge. This is a message addressed to the thousands of conscienceless enemies of the Muslims of India.
>
> TITLE: "Taking revenge is made compulsorily for us."
>
> Persecution/oppression in Gujarat was beyond tolerance of true Muslims. It was such an oppression that even devil would be astonished/not like to do.
>
> This oppression beyond tolerance has set ablaze hearts of Muslims with revenge and holy war. And few people have risen up for this revenge. When the blood of such Hindus and the blood of the police will flow, then the spirits of the martyred-killed in riots will rest in piece.
>
> Every young man of the movement Tehriq-e-Quasas will avenge for the Muslims martyred. Hindus will burn and pay for the martyred children, elderly, women, burnt houses and smoke of the burnt mosques. Representatives of Shiv

Sena, extremist sadhus of Vishwa Hindu Parishad and temples will burn, and only then martyred Muslims will rest in peace.

Come, come o Muslims of Gujarat, let's rebuild our mosques working shoulder to shoulder and matching steps with the young men of the Tehriq-e-Qasas. Let's avenge the martyrdom of Muslims. If we die let's die with respect, if we live it should be life of respect. This is for the betterment of the worldly life and the life beyond that. May Allah provide us with true leadership and keep Tehriq-e-Qasas alive till every martyr's death is avenged for. NOTE: Very soon we will take such actions that will prove that we are worthy heirs of those martyred in Gujarat. This is our gift to Advani and Modi. From now onward keep waiting. God willing.

WRITER: True representatives of the Muslims of Gujarat.

Needless to say, there was a certain lapse of time between the killing of the militants and the 'discovery' of the letter.

The murder of the Akshardham temple worshippers is the worst act of sectarian violence in Gujarat since the anti-Muslim riots left almost 1,500 people dead earlier this year. Over thirty civilians and police officers died, and many more are still in a serious condition in the Civil Hospitals of Gandhinagar and Ahmedabad. Women and children are among the victims.

One woman suffering from shrapnel wounds in the Civil Hospital in Ahmedabad confirmed that her two children died because of the attack.

The government was quick to point the finger at Muslim extremists and at Pakistan.

On September 25th, the Indian PM, Atal Behari Vajpayee, flew to Gandhinagar, visited the hospital and the Akshardham Temple, and spoke of Pakistan supporting terrorism. Gujarat's top official, Chief Minister Narendra Modi, blamed Islamic militants and Pakistan for the terror. The Foreign Minister, Yashwant Sinha, said that the methods used in the attack were similar to those employed in the assault on the Indian Parliament last December, an act that the Indian establishment blamed on Pakistan and almost led to war between the two nuclear powers.

The behavior of Indian politicians has been irresponsible. The two gunmen were not identified and the letter remains the only 'proof' linking the attackers to Muslim extremists. However, the letter does not mention Pakistan (or Kashmir). There is no doubt that the ruling BJP is following its own political agenda, seeking confrontation with its neighboring country and trying to justify its 'war on terrorism'.

Access to the survivors of the attack was, and remains, very limited. Members of the RSS are present in great numbers in both the Gujarati hospitals (the Civil Hospitals in Ahmedabad and Gandhinagar) where civilian victims and injured police officers are being treated. They listen to every word uttered by eyewitnesses to the press, often 'correcting' their statements.

The authorities reacted to the situation by deploying some three thousand troops in Gujarat in order to prevent incidents of violence and rioting similar to those that followed the February 27th attack on a train carrying Hindu nationalists. Those responsible for the attack were never identified, but most Hindus believe that Muslim extremists were to blame (although there is some speculation that extremists from the World Hindu Council (VHP) carried out the carnage themselves in order to fuel the conflict between Muslims and Hindus).

What followed was indiscriminate violence and rioting that targeted Muslim neighborhoods. Between 1,000 and 1,500 people died, hundreds of women were raped, one pregnant woman had her stomach split open, about thirty thousand houses were looted and destroyed, and Ahmedabad became a segregated city.

The local police force did very little to stop the violence and, in some instances, actively encouraged it.

After the temple incident, deployment of troops seemed to be the only sensible option since the army is still seen as neutral. This strategy shows some concern on the part of the politicians in Delhi and Gujarat to prevent the violence spiraling further out of control.

Despite all the preventive actions, tension is growing. A general strike called by Hindu nationalists shut down services in many parts of the country. Extremists threw stones and stopped several trains in Mumbai. In the Gujarati city of Surat, Hindu mobs stabbed two Muslim men, one as he was getting out of an auto rickshaw, and the other as he emerged from his house.

VHP's General Secretary, Mohan Salekar, delivered a chilling warning: "The strike is to warn that, if the government does not act in time, people will take the law into their own hands."

One day after the temple attack, new refugees started to arrive in the Muslim neighborhood of Vatva, on the outskirts of Ahmedabad. They were leaving Naroda Patiya and other the areas that were devastated in the riots earlier this year.

Shaja Bibi Sheikh, from Naroda Pathya, said, "Police told us to get out for two days." Her entire family of twelve people hit the road, moving to Vatva. "We were attacked during the riots and this time we don't want to wait until it happens again."

In Vatva, a fifteen-year-old boy named Javed spoke about the nine members of his close and extended family who were killed during the riots in Ahmedabad. He lost his mother, father and brother. He saw some of the killing and never fully recovered from the shock. He blames the police for failing to protect his relatives.

Dr. Vankar, a psychiatrist at the Civil Hospital of Ahmedabad, is Hindu, the co-author of the study 'Posttraumatic Stress Disorder in Riot Affected Women in Ahmedabad':

> I worked on this scientific study, but from a human perspective I can give you one example of what happened. A barber lived right next to my house. He and his two family members were killed during the riots. He was a simple, good man, and now he is no more. Always when I am passing his house, I

say to myself: "Here lived the barber, a Muslim, a gentle man who came from Uttar Pradesh searching for a better life. And they killed him."

As a motto for their report, doctors Khyati Mehta and G.K. Vankar chose a chilling poem by Aatish Bododvi:

Your city is like a burning courtyard. Your city is like a broken bangle, I do not intend to come to your city, I do not wish to come to your city.

Sabarmati Ashram in Ahmedabad was the starting point of Gandhi's 385 kilometre 'Salt March' to Dandi in March 1930. He vowed not to return to the Ashram until India gained independence.

Gandhi's philosophy of non-violence and secularism remains one of the most powerful symbols of modern India. However, Ahmedabad, where Gandhi lived for many years, is rapidly gaining a worldwide reputation for intolerance, religious conflict and acts of terror against innocent men, women and children.

The despicable murder of the worshippers in Gandhinagar can not be, nor should be, excused or forgiven. However, who was responsible is far from clear. Pointing fingers at the Muslim community and Pakistan will only aggravate an already tense situation. Even if, and there remains a big 'if', this attack was carried out by a small group of extreme fanatics of the Muslim faith, there should be no backlash against the local Muslim community that has already suffered enough injustice and horror in recent years and past decades.

Before this incident, Gujarat had already become a symbol of terror, not unlike Bosnia and Ambon. If the cycle of violence doesn't stop, it could destabilize the secular and democratic essence of the entire Indian nation.

October 20, 2002

The War Against Latin American Poor

For decades and centuries, Latin America has been the victim of terrorist acts conducted by the United States. Hundreds of thousands, maybe millions, have died in open and covert wars, ranging from the Mexican War to the unsuccessful coup against President Chavez of Venezuela. While officially 'free' and 'democratic', Latin American countries are, in reality, colonies with limited liberties, one of which is the freedom to elect their own governments, provided such governments are willing to fully cooperate with the United States and multinationals.

All attempts to create independent progressive governments have been ruthlessly suppressed, sometimes through direct intervention, sometimes by covert actions and terrorism, assassination plots, coups and economic blackmail. Cuba, the only country in Latin America to successfully defend its right to be different, has had to survive dozens of terrorist attacks conducted by its own exiles operating from US soil or directly executed by its northern neighbor.

For Latin America, the real White House 'axis of evil' (to use George W. Bush's own terminology, and not including the President himself) consists of three men employed by the US administration, Otto Juan Reich, John Negroponte and Elliot Abrams. All three were responsible for atrocities in Central America during the Reagan era, and have recently found their way back into the corridors of power in the present administration.

Otto Juan Reich, a right-wing Cuban-American obsessed with overthrowing Fidel Castro, was sworn in as the Assistant Secretary of State for Western Hemisphere Affairs on January 11, 2002. Reich is a close friend and supporter of Florida Governor Jeb Bush, the President's brother. He was discredited when his involvement in covert activities and misinformation tactics during the US interventions in Central America in the 80's and 90's came to public notice, but was unsurprisingly rehabilitated and embraced by the second Bush administration.

In his 'Latin America's Dilemma: Otto Reich's Propaganda is Reminiscent of the Third Reich', Tom Turnipseed (ZNet April 18, 2002) wrote:

> On September 30, 1987, a Republican appointed comptroller general of the U.S. found that Reich had done things as director of the OPD (State Department's Office of Public Diplomacy) that were 'prohibited covert propaganda activities...'. The same report said Mr. Reich's operation violated 'a restriction on the State Department's annual appropriations prohibiting the use of federal funds for publicity or propaganda purposes not authorized by Congress.' Reich used covert propaganda to demonize the democratically elected Sandinista government of Nicaragua and establish the Contras as fearless freedom fighters. The purpose was to make the U.S. public afraid enough of the Sandinistas to get Congress to fund the Contras directly. The Boland Amendment was

passed by Congress in 1982 that prohibited U.S. funds from being used to overthrow the Nicaraguan government. Meanwhile, the Contras were being illegally armed by the Reagan administration via the Iran-Contra arms deal... On the night of Reagan's re-election in 1984, Reich's office put out the news that 'intelligence sources' revealed that Soviet MIG fighter jets were arriving in Nicaragua and Andrea Mitchell interrupted election night coverage on NBC to give the phoney report. This resembles Joseph Goebbel's fabrication that Polish troops had attacked German soldiers to give the Third Reich an excuse to launch the Nazi blitzkrieg into Poland to begin World War II in 1939. Other Reich prevarications given to media sources included: Nicaragua had been given chemical weapons by the Soviets, according to the Miami Herald; and leaders of the Sandinistas were involved in drug trafficking, according to Newsweek magazine.

Reich, former US ambassador to Venezuela and close associate of Mobil Oil when in the country, began his role as Assistant Secretary of State by attempting to discredit the left-wing Venezuelan President Hugo Chavez, accusing him of supporting the Colombian FARC guerrillas and tampering with the independent, but state-owned, oil company.

Reich was involved in the failed anti-Chavez coup in Venezuela. According to Ed Vulliamy (The Guardian, April 22, 2002):

> Reich is said by Organization of American States (OAS) sources to have had a number of meetings

> with Carmona (leader of the coup and right-wing Venezuelan businessman) and other leaders of the coup over several months. The coup was discussed in some detail, right down to its timing and chances of success, which were deemed excellent.... On the day Carmona claimed power, Reich summoned ambassadors from Latin America and the Caribbean to his office. He said the removal of Chavez was not a rupture of democratic rule, as he had resigned and was 'responsible for his fate'. He said the US would support the Carmona government.

Reich hosted Venezuelan right-wing leaders, including Carmona himself, on several occasions prior to the failed coup.

Elliott Abrams was appointed as 'a senior director of the National Security Council for democracy, human rights and international operations' by the second Bush administration.

Probably the most sinister of the three, Abrams used to be one of the leading theoreticians of the school of thought known as 'Hemispherism'. The main purpose of this 'philosophy' was to fight Marxism in the Americas, and support extreme right-wing regimes and death squads in Guatemala, El Salvador, Honduras and Argentina as well as the 1973 military coup against Salvador Allende in Chile.

In July 2, 2001 David Corn of 'The Nation' wrote:

> 'How would you feel if your wife and children were brutally raped before being hacked to death by soldiers during a military massacre of 800

civilians, and then two governments tried to cover up the killing?' It's a question that won't be asked of Elliott Abrams at a Senate confirmation hearing – because George W. Bush, according to press reports, may appoint Abrams to a National Security Council staff position that (conveniently!) does not require Senate approval.... One Abrams specialty was massacre denial. During a *Nightline* appearance in 1985, he was asked about reports that the US-funded Salvadoran military had slaughtered civilians at two sites the previous summer. Abrams maintained that no such events had occurred.... Three years earlier, when two American journalists reported that an elite, US-trained military unit had massacred hundreds of villagers in El Mozote, Abrams told Congress that the story was commie propaganda, as he fought for more US aid to El Salvador's military. The massacre, as has since been confirmed, was real. And in 1993, after a UN truth commission had examined 22,000 atrocities that occurred during the twelve-year war in El Salvador and attributed 85 percent of the abuses to the Reagan-assisted right-wing military and its death-squad allies, Abrams declared "The Administration's record on El Salvador is one of fabulous achievement...." But it wasn't his lies about mass murder that got Abrams into trouble. After a Contra re-supply plane was shot down in 1986, Abrams, one of the coordinators of Reagan's pro-Contra policy (along with the NSC's Oliver North and the CIA's Alan Fiers), appeared several times before a Congressional committee and withheld information on the Administration's connection to the secret and private Contra-support network. He also hid from Congress the fact that he had flown to London (using the name of "Mr. Kenilworth") to solicit a $10 million contribution for the Contras from the Sultan of Brunei. At the subsequent closed-door hearing, Democratic Senator Thomas Eagleton blasted Abrams for having misled legislators, noting that Abrams's misrepresentation could lead to 'slammer time'. Abrams disagreed, saying, 'You've heard my testimony.' Eagleton cut in: 'I've heard it, and I want to puke.'

Abrams is thought to be the man who gave the green light to the failed coup against President Hugo Chavez of Venezuela.

John D. Negroponte was confirmed by the Senate as the Permanent United States Representative to the United Nations on September 14, 2001 and sworn in on September 18, 2001.

An uncompromising right-winger and anti-Communist, Negroponte used to be Ambassador to Honduras, the Philippines and Mexico. While he was Reagan's Ambassador to Honduras (1981-1985), a US-trained death squad (Battalion 3-16) killed and tortured members of the alleged opposition. He was involved in forming the Contras, a paramilitary right-wing army that terrorized Nicaraguans in an attempt to bring down the Marxist Sandinista government. The US-backed Contras mostly operated from Honduran territory.

Three hard-line cold-warriors, three criminals who couldn't get decent positions even in the first Bush government or the later Clinton administration, are now rehabilitated and back in the saddle, ready to spread terror all over the continent.

Latin America is once again being (openly) treated as a colony. Michael Marx McCarthy, lead researcher of the influential 'Council on Hemispheric Affairs' (COHA, founded in 1975) writes that: "...the nomination of Abrams, Negroponte and Reich... has elicited hemispheric-wide criticism that the US has regressed to outmoded cold war politics when it comes to Latin America..."

One of the first 'political' acts toward Latin America by the second Bush administration was ruthless interference in the Nicaraguan electoral process in 2001. Openly favouring right-wing parties, the US unleashed a powerful propaganda campaign against Sandinista candidate Daniel Ortega and his party. In one of his colourful statements, Oliver Garza, the US ambassador to Managua, openly declared that if Ortega won, the US would return to the same foreign policy for Nicaragua as in the past, referring to the illegal (even by the US standards) support for the terrorist 'Contra' groups that devastated Nicaraguan during the Sandinista government.

The US also warned that a Sandinista victory and an Ortega government would have disastrous financial consequences for the country. For his part, US State Department official Lino Gutierrez successfully urged right-wing parties to bury their differences, unite and defeat Daniel Ortega.

At the same time, the US escalated its involvement in Colombia, a South American country torn asunder by a bitter civil war. On top of two billion dollars pledged to support 'Plan Colombia', a scheme by which money is directed toward the Colombian state and military closely connected to the murderous right-wing paramilitary forces fighting left-wing guerrillas, President Alvaro Uribe Velez is getting a further 800 million dollars for the military and for protecting an oil pipeline. His administration is building a million-strong network of civilian informants, while arming peasants to create what may become yet another paramilitary force. Ignoring accusations and warnings from several human rights groups that Uribe (sworn in on August 7th, 2002) is himself linked to the paramilitaries, the US fully embraced the Colombian President's determination to break off negotiations with left-wing rebels until they disarm unilaterally. Uribe, adopting the language of his masters, is promising a 'full scale war on terror'.

Uribe's father was allegedly killed by the FARC for refusing to abandon his farm during land-redistribution. It is widely believed that Uribe's thirst for revenge is his main political motivator. Even his close friends are uncertain about his motives. "I was Uribe's classmate, his close friend," I was told by medical doctor Juan Antonio Correa M. from Medellin. "I voted for him because the situation in Colombia is so disastrous. But did I have second thoughts? You bet I did…"

In the meantime, the US is continuing to use chemical warfare to target coca crops in Putumayo and elsewhere, indifferent to the fact that such activities destroy everything else growing in the vicinity.

Plan Colombia is only the tip of an iceberg. The entire region is entering an intensive period of militarization that has its roots in the Clinton years. The US military presence in Latin America is increasing: in many cases, there are attempts to bring local armies under direct US military control. The construction of 'Forward Operating Locations' (FOL's) is increasing in the region. Currently there are FOLs in Ecuador, Aruba, Curacao and the Dutch Antilles, with a new addition in El Salvador. FOLs are small US military bases that are being set up in 'strategically important areas' to supplement existing larger bases. The Northern parts of South America, Colombia and Venezuela under its revolutionary President Hugo Chavez, are especially vulnerable to the military plans of United States.

The construction of a giant US satellite launcher and an adjacent airport in the jungle of Guyana, the eastern neighbor of Venezuela, almost led to a breaking-off of diplomatic relations between the two countries. There are presently no flights between the two capitals. The US claims that the satellite launcher is designed for strictly peaceful uses, but government sources in Caracas claim that it could easily be converted into a military installation in no time at all.

The US involvement in the coup to overturn left-wing Venezuelan President Hugo Chavez sent a shiver down the spine of the entire continent. While the President was being arrested by a group of rebellious soldiers serving the interests of the business elite in Caracas and Maracaibo, media outlets controlled by big business continued to spread lies and false reports. In Reich's tradition, the US State Department reacted to the coup by issuing the following communiqué:

> …The Venezuelan military commendably refused to fire on peaceful demonstrators, and the media valiantly kept the Venezuelan public informed.… Yesterday's events in Venezuela resulted in a transitional government until new elections can be held. Though details are still unclear, undemocratic actions committed or encouraged by the Chavez

administration provoked yesterday's crisis in Venezuela....

Later, hundreds of thousands of Venezuelans took to the streets demanding the return of the President for whom they had voted in democratic elections. The US State Department scaled down its rhetoric, denying its involvement in the plot to depose Chavez. Too late, however: by then the US stance on the issue had become abundantly clear!

After returning to the Presidential palace, Hugo Chavez and members of his cabinet ordered an investigation and accused foreign powers of intervening in their country's domestic affairs.

One of the most scandalous US interventions in Latin America in recent years occurred in Bolivia, the poorest South American country, where the leftist anti-globalist Evo Morales achieved an amazing electoral performance by finishing second in the Presidential elections with 20.94 percent of the vote, only just behind Gonzalo Sanchez de Lozado, a rich businessman, who received 22.46 percent.

Evo Morales, from the 'Movement Toward Socialism' (MAS), became famous as a leader of the coca growers unions that were opposing a US-backed eradication campaign which was deepening the poverty of many Bolivian farmers. Morales had been expelled from the Congress earlier in the year for his involvement with the radical farmers who had confronted the police, killing three officers. It is widely believed that the US was behind his expulsion.

Although confronting the US and the corrupt Bolivian elite gained Morales, an indigenous Aymara, enormous popularity at home, he became a victim of vitriolic propaganda in the US media. The US Ambassador, Manuel Rocha, urged Bolivians not to vote for Morales, threatening that if did, the US would withdraw its aid. On the Wednesday before the elections, he declared: "As a representative of the United States, I want to remind the Bolivian electorate that, if you elect those who want Bolivia to become a major cocaine exporter again, this will endanger the future of U.S. assistance to Bolivia…"

The wording of Rocha's statement is misleading. Morales did not intend to turn Bolivia into 'a major cocaine exporter'. In fact, he is against drug trafficking, a view he repeated many times during his election campaign.

He defends the cultivation of coca leaf as a plant that is important for millions of poor farmers in the Bolivian and Peruvian Andes. Coca was integral to the cultural rituals in the Inca Empire and before. It is still legal in both Bolivia and Peru – coca teabags are clearly stamped and labelled as 'Industria Peruana' or 'Industria Boliviana'. Living high in the 'altiplano', sometimes more than 4,000m above sea level, local people chew coca leaves to fight fatigue, hunger and altitude sickness. Coca leaf is not a narcotic: if chewed or drunk as tea it has a very mild effect, not unlike that of tobacco or coffee. Cocaine and its cheaper and deadlier derivatives such as 'crack' are produced by an extremely complicated chemical process in permanent or mobile laboratories based Colombia, Paraguay and other countries. Such laboratories do not operate on Bolivian territory.

For many years, Latin Americans have argued that the 'war on drugs' should be fought on the demand side in the US itself.

However, the United States prefers to fight a 'supply side' war, using indiscriminate chemical fumigation that destroys not only the coca plants, but everything else that grows nearby, thereby threatening the livelihood of poor farmers and their families. The 'war' plunges farmers into even deeper misery, for promises to provide substantial aid if they choose to change their crops exist only on paper. Those who gain from this policy are the local military forces who are the main recipients of the US support. Almost inevitably, countries that have cooperated with the US war on drugs have experienced an increase in human rights violations.

The 'war on drugs' often serves to conceal US regional military involvement in countries such as Colombia, Peru and Bolivia. For instance, in Colombia the main goal is to destroy the FARC guerrilla movement that the US accuses of drug smuggling, while ignoring the extensive illegal drug trafficking carried out by the Colombian armed forces and paramilitaries.

One consistent feature of the US wars in Latin America is a complete disregard for the plight of poor people. Almost without exception, the US sides with rich and oligarchic elites, and opposes popular leaders, movements and governments. Historically, the predominantly white Latin American business and political elite has maintained close ties with the US and Europe and, more recently, with multinational companies.

The US appears to be willing to do practically anything to support the 'elites' of Latin American: arranging coups, funding death-squads, helping to 'fix' elections, even mobilizing direct military intervention. As long as these feudal elites hold power, there is no danger that multinational companies will lose their grip on a continent that has been plundered by foreign interests for over five hundred years.

It is hard to find a country in Latin America that has not been terrorized by the consequences of the Monroe doctrine. Mexico lost almost half its territory, Guatemala, Honduras, Nicaragua and El Salvador experienced the horror of US-backed death squads, Cuba survived an embargo, terrorist attacks and direct invasions, and Panama and Nicaragua were occupied. There were coups against democratically elected politicians and governments in Chile, Bolivia and the Dominican Republic, and bloodthirsty regimes in Argentina, Brazil and Uruguay received full support. The list goes on…!

So far, no US administration has moved to review its policy toward Latin America. Some administrations were, of course, worse than others: Bill Clinton, often hailed by centrists for his soft approach toward the south, laid the foundations for Plan Colombia and extending the US military presence in Latin America, including extending the FOLs mentioned earlier. However, his actions can hardly be compared to the inhumanity and bandit-style cynicism with which the Reagan administration handled hemispheric affairs. Experience to date suggests that the present administration may be even worse.

Although accounts of the crimes committed by the US in Latin America would fill many books, remembering the past is considered radical in the majority of Latin American countries. Those who are willing to talk about the victims of the 1973 coup in Chile, and the dictatorship that followed it, are immediately marked as leftists and therefore not 'mainstream'. All over Latin America, only the radical left is concerned to raise the issue of US involvement in the coup against Chavez. The South American dominant media usually mention the phenomenon of death squads in Central America as a chain of secondary events connected with the Cold War. Dozens of influential writers and analysts, from Alvaro Vargas Llosa, the son of Maria Vargas Llosa and co-author of the 'Manual of Perfect Latin American Idiot' (an appalling book that accuses the Latin American poor of bringing the continent to its present devastated state) and ending with Jorge Castaneda, the Mexican Minister of Foreign Affairs, are offering a distorted view. Typically, this is designed to lull their compatriots into believing that, despite everything that has happened, their continent is on the right course, and probably always was.

Nevertheless, the war against the poor continues and is accelerating under the present US administration and its advisors. This covert war, often described in the North as 'spreading democracy', the 'war against terrorism', or the 'war on drugs', will not stop until there is an awareness in both Latin America and in the US that it exists. At present, the US public is largely unaware of what is happening, and the reality is only just beginning to infiltrate the consciousness of people in Latin America.

August 2002

North Korea: Who's Afraid Of Whom

Is the world in general, and Asia in particular, really trembling? Is North Korea, one of the countries on the infamous US hit list with the mystical name of 'Axis of Evil', really frightening everyone?

Asian capitals seem to be far from horror-struck. Weeks after North Korean 'Dear Leader', Kim Jong Il, allegedly admitted that Pyongyang was continuing its nuclear program, which almost everybody else had known or suspected for years, nothing has changed.

Washington claims that North Korea has breached the 1994 nuclear arms control agreement, in which it promised not to develop nuclear weapons. This accusation is based on a vague (alleged) admission by Pyongyang, in October, that it has a uranium-enriching program that would allow it to produce nuclear weapons.

The Russians, historic allies of North Korea, asked Pyongyang for clarification of the situation, which was presented at the end of October by Pak Ui Chun, the country's Ambassador to Moscow. Subsequently, while rebuking Pyongyang for 'ambiguous language', Russia pointed out that what North Korea had presented to the US was "neither admission, nor denial" of the existence of a nuclear program. The Tokyo, Singapore and Hong Kong authorities are definitely not planning to convert their subway systems into underground nuclear bunkers following this revelation. Hordes of scared Asians leaving for safer and distant shores are nowhere in sight. Massive anti-North Korean popular demonstrations are non-existent. In truth, hardly anyone in Asia Pacific cares much about the hermit state's nukes. Finding someone that thinks North Korea intends full-scale aggression against nearby states is almost impossible. On the other hand, plenty of people in the region can well remember two earlier aggressors – the Western nations and Japan.

Of course, some politicians are punctilious in their duty to express to the world's rulers their concern, disappointment, even outrage over Kim's (alleged) confessional outpouring. Statements condemning North Korea periodically appear on the front pages of major newspapers in Japan, South Korea and elsewhere in the region.

Behind the official rhetoric, the situation in the region is calm. Asian countries are not mobilizing their reservists, and there is no talk of significant increases in their military budgets.

Last week, Japan, South Korea and, of course, the US, issued a joint statement insisting that North Korea cease its nuclear program. Pyongyang promised to consider the demand if Washington concluded a non-aggression treaty with North Korea. Predictably, the North Koreans didn't forget to accuse the US of escalating the conflict.

People in the Far East seem to be as unconcerned about North Korea as most of those in the Middle East countries are about any present day threat from Iraq and Iran, two more of Washington's "Axis of Evil."

Asia has no significant historical reason to fear North or South Korea. Korea is known to be a peaceful nation. Although it fought a bitter civil war, with massive US involvement, between 1950 and 1953, never in modern history has it tried to intervene in the affairs of other nations. Furthermore, the people of Korea have never dropped nukes on anybody. Modern day Korea has no legacy of colonization of vast Asian land areas and hasn't attempted to impose a foreign-designed world order on the rest of the planet.

Unless the US and its faithful servants in the region come up with an enormously influential propaganda pitch, supported by another bunch of 'secret' files that cannot be exposed to the eyes of the public for 'national security' reasons, it will be very difficult to convince Asian people that North Korea should be 'punished' or invaded.

Observed from across the Pacific, North Korea seems to be almost completely isolated. In reality, it has solid ties with several Asian nations and with Russia. Its relations with China are also increasingly positive – there is no doubt that China will play the most important role in the recently announced reforms that will include several 'free market zones' in the border area. Vietnam and North Korea are old friends and allies and the private guard of Cambodian King Sihanouk consists exclusively of North Koreans.

Further evidence of warming international relationships is a specially designated tourist area (served by "Hyundai's Kumgangsan Tours), developed by South Korean companies, which can be now visited by foreigners. Reconstruction of the railroad connecting the North and South of Korea is in progress. If the proposed construction of an undersea tunnel between Japan and Korea goes ahead, South Korean and Japanese goods and passengers will have easy access to China and Europe. All this doesn't yet amount to much, but it is definitely something at least.

In recent months, North Korea has been tentatively beginning to open up. It should be encouraged in its efforts, not be constantly forced onto the defensive and made to feel threatened.

Possession of nuclear weapons by any state should not be welcomed. But then again, why should one worry more about one or two North Korean nukes (and that's only if Kim Jong Il is not just bragging) than about the far larger arsenals of the former colonial, and present neo-colonial, powers – empires that have been plundering enormous tracts of Asia from Malaya to Indochina, from the Urals to Sakhalin, for centuries?

Doesn't North Korea, a country that has suffered a terrible Japanese occupation and, later, a brutal war fueled by the United States and, once again, by Japan, have more justification to be concerned about the US military bases just a few hundred miles away in Okinawa and elsewhere? These bases are equipped with countless nuclear missiles and other weapons of mass destruction, all targeted at points all over the Asian continent. Neither Japan nor the United States has previously hesitated to use such military might, with many countries in Asia, including Korea, as their victims.

Taking the country's past into account, it wouldn't be too daring to claim that North Korea has reason to worry about its safety. After all, there are still thirty-seven thousand heavily armed US troops stationed on the border separating the two Koreas!

Are we afraid of a North Korean nuclear arsenal only because we disagree with its political and economic system?

North Korea is definitely not one of the world's most pleasant countries to live in. Nor do its leaders have many scruples, as shown by several cases of kidnapped Japanese citizens. Pyongyang is not exactly overindulging its citizens, nor can be hardly called a champion of pluralism and democracy.

Nevertheless, North Korea is no worse than the succession of fascist regimes that we in the West have supported since the Second World War. It has many more reasons to be afraid of us, of the US and of Japanese imperialist tendencies, than we have to fear its primitive uranium-enrichment program.

November 2002

Amnesia In Rhodes

After 9-11 and the subsequent US threat of crusades against those who are "not with us," the Island of Rhodes was often on my mind.

It seemed inevitable that the Western world would soon try again, directly or indirectly, to bring most independent political systems, economies and cultures of the world to heel. However, I hoped, I even believed, that some small island of sanity, of beauty and of kindness, had to exist somewhere, a place where Western values at their best were still surviving intact.

My guess was that Rhodes – the oldest, continuously inhabited medieval city in Europe – had to be exactly such a place. I had been dreaming of the old city of Lindos, with its whitewashed houses, ancient ruins, olive groves and local bars – places where men and women were still obsessed with passionate discussions about world events, the death of genuine democracy, and the dictatorial, terrorist tendencies of the so called 'civilized world'.

In December, the UN inspectors were still in Baghdad, searching presidential palaces, but Bush and his administration were getting increasingly hawkish. Although there seemed to be no reason for war, we were told by the servile press that war "seems to be inevitable." No solutions to the Middle East conflict seemed to be in sight. There was a new threat of famine in Africa. Hugo Chavez, the democratically elected President of Venezuela, was under fire from the right wing business elite in Venezuela and those it had managed to indoctrinate.

I felt I was ready to discuss politics, philosophy and democracy with the true descendents of those who believed that all people, not just economic elites, should be ruling the world.

So, one day I booked my ticket to Rhodes, all the way from Japan, via Vienna and Athens.

I flew to Rhodes and drove to Lindos, anticipating a great intellectual adventure. There were almost no tourists in December, so it was easy to find a small room in an old house, overlooking the ruins of the ancient Greek theatre.

The same night that I arrived, Lindos exploded in a spontaneous fiesta. Local men brought musical instruments to several bars and restaurants, delicious food was passed on huge plates, and homemade wine was flowing from countless barrels and bottles. People drank and sang, and doors were open to everyone. "What are you doing here in December?" I was asked. "Nobody comes at this time of the year. The water is almost too cold to swim in, and the dance halls and discos are closed."

I explained that I had come to discuss philosophy, democracy and the world order.

They looked at me in disbelief. They definitely thought I was weird. "Have some wine," they said.

I did. Then, in the corner of a tavern I raised an issue of US foreign policy.

"Have some more wine," they insisted. It was hard to refuse.

Someone brought a bottle of chilled white wine and filled my glass: "Here in Rhodes, we don't care much about politics. For half a year, we have so many foreign tourists that we can hardly move. Almost everyone on the island lives from tourism. In the winter, almost all of us do nothing. We just enjoy life or travel abroad. We close down stores, restaurants, pubs, everything."

I mentioned Iraq, but they shut me up. Iraq was definitely not a popular topic in Rhodes. I asked about democracy, about the way they see representative democracies in Western Europe and in the US degenerating into its present shameful form.

"One has to study democracy in order to understand it," said someone, offering his opinion. It was around 3 a.m.

"Don't think too much," someone else told me. "Enjoy the island. Enjoy your vacation."

But I was not on vacation.

The World Heritage city of Rhodes really was shut down. In the summer, it probably looked like one enormous souvenir store, shopping and entertainment district, and historic museum, all rolled into one. Alternatively, maybe it looked like historical Disneyland. Now, in the winter, the hydrofoils were grounded, most of the cafes and hotels were closed, and information was unavailable. The city looked too unnatural, too well and too recently restored – too perfect, too European.

I drove all over the island, putting over 400 miles on my little lazy rented car. In five days, I didn't stumble across one single bookstore, contemporary art gallery or DVD store selling independent films. Internet cafes were few and well hidden.

Lunch in a local restaurant was going for almost twenty Euros, without wine, in a country where an average income still hardly reaches one thousand Euros. Coffee, orange juice and a little toast could set you back almost ten Euros. EU flags were hanging on dozens of buildings and souvenir shops, now closed for the winter. Countless stores were decorated with "Wir sprechen Deutch" and "We speak English."

Some streets in the delightful small towns had been given the names of great ancient Greek philosophers and writers, but philosophy had become something not worth discussing. Foreign politics had disappeared from the radar, unless Turkey or Macedonia was involved.

During my visit to Rhodes, millions of men, women and children all over the world were facing starvation. Western terror was increasing, sometimes in obvious, sometimes in hidden form.

Greece itself experienced this terror twice in its recent history: its occupation during WWII and the US backed military dictatorship after the war.

I made dozens of attempts to discuss philosophy, foreign affairs and democracy with the local men and women. I failed. Only once did I come close, talking to my landlady a few miles from the ancient city of Kamiros. "You would enjoy talking to my daughter," she said. "She reads books and she is questioning our political system." I asked where I could find her. "She left for Boston," came the answer. "But she has an Internet address."

Apart from its breathtaking scenery, excellent olive oil, tomatoes, wine and music, Greece will soon be indistinguishable from any other EU country. As with almost all European countries, it is now suffering from political apathy.

I got no answers in Rhodes. But I was asked many questions by local people (after they learned that I live and work in Asia). Some wanted to know which Japanese writer wrote the Kama Sutra, how many people die every year from hunger in Thailand, or when the Cambodian civil war was going to come to an end. One older man expressed deep concern over the fragility of the peace between the Tamil Tigers and the government of Laos.

"We hate Germans, but we cannot live without them," confessed the owner of one bar in Lindos. "Honestly speaking, we generally hate tourists. But thanks to them, we can work only six months a year and the rest of the time…"

"Discuss philosophy and politics?" I interrupted with a dose of irony.

"Get out of here," he laughed. "Who cares about that crap? The rest of the time we just do nothing, or travel to Australia. Or stuff like that…"

I left Rhodes. Before departing from Greece, I spent one night in the old neighborhood of Plaka, in Athens. I went to several DVD shops, ready to buy films by my favorite Greek director, Costa Garvas. They knew his name, but carried not one of his films.

Greece is heading full-speed toward complete integration with the European Union. I noticed that it was too busy digesting its calories; too busy trying on suddenly affordable designer clothes, to pay attention to me.

To most inhabitants of Rhodes, the rest of the world seemed to be far away. Suddenly I had no doubt that we will have to find our own answers, and exorcise our own demons across the Atlantic, without counting too much on help from the old world.

January 2003

Self Censorship In The US

Not Unlike The Soviet Version

An attack against Iraq seems to be inevitable. No matter what Iraq does, no matter what the UN arms inspectors say or find (or don't find), the US administration is apparently determined to invade. Once again it will 'level the ground' (or blow sky high) yet another poor and basically defenseless nation in the name of 'civilized values' such as freedom and democracy.

While Bush, members of his administration and his advisors (most of them hardly a bunch of olive branch carrying peacemakers) speak about peace and freedom, "our values" and "civilization," they are, in reality, simply carrying out the long and brutal traditions of Western expansionism to an extreme.

The administration is tampering with language on a daily basis. Words that, for centuries, were sacred to millions of people all over the world are suddenly turning into meaningless clichés, into the empty slogans of the propaganda machine.

The government-spread propaganda is mostly primitive, sometimes even comical. It almost begs to be ridiculed. However, both the US and European dominant media are exercising incredible restraint and self discipline, ready to swallow almost everything that it is given by the policymakers and top military brass on both sides of Atlantic. It is becoming a well-groomed poodle, touchingly attached to its two masters, the big business that owns it and governments that serve the interests of big business. It has lost its ability to criticize, its sense of humor and its sarcastic edge. And it is hardly a secret that the use of humor, irony and sarcasm is one of the main fears of any manipulative establishment.

Many of my honorable friends and colleagues in the United States (those who are refusing to become blind and servile) are outraged and shocked. I am outraged, too, but not shocked. To me, it all feels just too familiar: I experienced a similar situation many years ago, as a child growing up in what used to be known as the 'Soviet bloc'.

I grew up in the sixties and seventies in what was then the Czechoslovak Socialist Republic, in a city at the Western extreme of the country, known for its beer and heavy industry – Pilsen.

Despite its proximity to the West (Pilsen is just fifty kilometers from Bavaria as the crow flies), Western

Bohemia, as well as other regions of the country, had to absorb a continuous barrage of official propaganda channeled through the state television, radio and censored newspapers and magazines.

Today, nobody has any doubts that the state-controlled media in the former Soviet bloc countries were bombarding millions of people with simplifications, half-truths and outright lies.

Lies were printed and broadcast every day. The only (very positive) difference from the present situation in the West was that nobody seemed to pay much attention. Nearly every night, I fell asleep to the sound of the news bulletins broadcast by the BBC World Service (in English, since the Czech language bulletins were sometimes jammed). Television sets in almost every household were tuned to the West German ARD or ZDF, and teenagers were rocking and rolling to the sound of the latest hits from Radio Luxemburg or Bavaria3. Books by Sartre, Camus, Beckett and other influential Western thinkers were available in libraries, although one had to search for them. Cinemas and film clubs were showing most of the important world productions with only one or two year delays.

If it was an intellectual hell, we were growing up in its first class compartment!

Newspapers and magazines were boring and dull: most of us bought them just for their crossword puzzles and the latest film and concert listings. It was obvious that the journalists writing for them didn't believe a word that they were writing – it was just another job, another way to collect a higher than average state salary, to get by, to survive. In those days, published journalists had dubious reputations as intellectual prostitutes. Those who wrote for the official press were mostly spineless and mediocre men and women, lacking self-respect and professional honor. There was no sarcasm, no irony, nor creative edge in what they did. They wrote what was expected of them. Then they went home. Twice a month they got paid. Many of them hit the bottle.

Later, being obsessed with one simple question: 'how did the censorship of those years really work?' I spoke to several former journalists. I was surprised to learn that there were no fat, sadistic censors standing behind them – far from it!

"To be honest with you, there were no censors in sight," explained one former editor of an important daily in Prague. "We knew what we had to write, what the party line was. We knew our limits when we wanted to criticize something. Nobody had to bother to stand behind our back. We censured ourselves."

In fact, journalists were expected to be critical of the system. They were encouraged to bash low-level corruption and other minor negative elements of the system. As long as they kept reminding their readers that the system itself was superior, they were on the right track.

There were no gulags in Czechoslovakia in the sixties and seventies, no concentration camps, no torture chambers. Those who crossed the line by choosing honesty and professionalism were not kidnapped. Parents of dissidents were not tortured before their eyes. There were no extra-judicial executions (unlike in our colonies in, say, Central America). Those who decided to tell the truth simply lost their jobs, became unemployable or were forced to become manual workers or window washers. Only a few of those who decided to stand against the system were imprisoned. They included several dissidents, among them Vaclav Havel.

The system in Czechoslovakia functioned almost flawlessly. Extreme violence was unnecessary. Fear of losing privileges did the trick. Almost all journalists knew their duties: they knew what was expected from them. Mostly they didn't have to be told what to think and what to write: they knew it intuitively. They may have lacked integrity, but they weren't stupid, after all. And they had families to feed and houses to furnish!

Does it sound familiar?

Some twenty years later, the situation is not so different in my adoptive homeland – the United States. If we decide to tell the truth, to write about the lies and manipulation of our government, to challenge the very essence of our system, we are not risking kidnapping, torture or assassination. We will still be able to wake up in the morning in our own bed, to drink a cup of coffee at the corner coffee shop, to take a walk. But our lives may nevertheless change dramatically. Chances are that we will encounter evasive answers from otherwise friendly editors of the magazines that we used to write for periodically, and the number of work related emails will dramatically decrease. Soon, we will have to look for another job. We will still be able to write for progressive publications (one major difference from the situation in the former Soviet bloc), but it will not bring in enough funds to pay for our rent in cities like New York or Boston.

I understand why some of my colleagues decided to collaborate with the Bush administration and his crusaders. I disagree with those who did, but I understand nevertheless. Choices are hard to make. Many "official" journalists and analysts (we can now call them this) have families, their children have to go to colleges, and mortgages have to be paid. It is more comfortable to suffer during the morning rush hour in the leather seat of the brand new Saab, than to wait for the commuter bus on the way to the end of the unemployment line.

The Czech system (or call it 'regime' if you prefer) was not particularly rich, but it was able to offer some privileges to those who were seeking them in exchange for loyalty and servility. Our system today is decisively wealthier: it could and would happily buy us all if we were ready to put ourselves on sale. And it is ready to supply us with so many succulent, tasty carrots that we could easily munch on them for the rest of our lives.

Our country is extremely rich (as are our allies in Europe and Asia). It can offer limitless privileges and a high life to those who decide to play according to the rules – rules that are lately becoming much stricter, by the way. If we refuse to play the game, we will probably not be hit brutally by the stick – the system will simply withhold the carrots.

For some of us, the price of collaboration is simply too high. We would have to hold on to our sarcasm until we reached the door of our neighborhood bar. We would have to overlook the fate of millions, probably billions of men, women and children who are suffering all over the world as a consequence of our brutally-enforced interests. We would have to call war 'a peace', aggression 'a defense', lies 'a truth'. We would have to bend our own beliefs and learn how to avoid eye contact with those who had chosen to remain true to their principles.

But if we decide to tell the truth the way we see it, we should do it without feelings of superiority and self-congratulation. In many ways, in our own ways, we are privileged, too. We are enjoying the true freedom that comes with being 'outside the game'. We don't have to re-read our own articles over and over again, nor be scared that our work could contain some sentences displeasing to those whose interests we would be paid to defend. After all, what can give greater joy to a writer than being able to tell the truth to the best of his or her ability, to express his or her own beliefs, to speak his or her own mind, to refuse to indulge in humiliating self-censorship?

I don't think we should be too harsh on our colleagues in the US and Europe who have decided to compromise themselves. Some are forced to do so by circumstances. Some, like so many in former Czechoslovakia, do it in order to provide for their families.

But neither should we forget the simple words of Czech poet Jaroslav Seifert, laureate of the Nobel Price for Literature, a man of lyrical verse, who once failed to contain his frustration and barked at the full session of the Union of Czech writers: "The writer should be the conscience of his own nation.... If anyone else omits, or decides not to pronounce the truth, it can be understood: it can be simply considered as a tactical maneuver. If the writer withholds the truth, he is a liar."

January 2003

Asia And The War With Iraq

In February, the people of Asia stood shoulder to shoulder, protesting in front of their US embassies against the forthcoming war against Iraq. They marched through rain, snow and tropical heat, their numbers varying from several hundreds to hundreds of thousands. But their message was unanimous: "We are not irrelevant. We, the people of the largest and the most populous continent on earth are against the war and against Western hegemony. And we want our voices to be heard."

Even in Japan, a country often described as the staunchest supporter of US foreign policy, around 80 percent of the population is against the war. There is no major nation on the Asian continent that is cheering for an invasion of Iraq.

From Indonesia to Iran, from Japan to Sri Lanka, people are asking the same question: who gave the moral mandate to the United States and the rest of the Western world to preside over the fate of the country that is located thousands of miles from their national boundaries?

Asian unity on the issue of war against Iraq was clearly visible during the summit of Non-Aligned Nations in Kuala Lumpur. The Non-Aligned Movement unites 116 countries: two-thirds of the countries that make up the United Nations. The great majority of Asian nations are also members of the NAM.

Malaysian PM, Mahathir Mohamad, declared "…the uncertainties of today's world are due not to 'a clash of civilizations' between the West and Islam, but to a revival of the old European trait of wanting to dominate the world. The expression of this trait invariably involves injustices and oppression of people of other ethnic origins and colors. It is no longer just a war against terrorism. It is, in fact, a war to dominate the world."

While the newspapers in Southeast Asia were full of quotes from Mohathir's speeches, the Western media exhibited a profound disinterest and disrespect to the opinion of people from the great majority of the world, openly expressed by their leaders at the summit of NAM.

"The West talks about some disagreements between the US and Germany and between the US and France," said a painter in Ubud (he didn't want to be identified), a small town on the Hindu island of Bali.

"These Western countries have just some small disagreements. They all say that Iraq has to comply with their will and that it has to disarm, they just differ in their views about how it should be achieved. In the end, France and Germany will not defend Iraq from US aggression. We in Asia say: the West terrorized this continent for centuries and, in many ways, still does. We all suffered more from Europeans than from Iraqis. Why should we now listen to the West? It has no moral mandate, no right to define for all of us what is right and what is wrong."

"Since the demise of the Soviet Union, the 'other superpower' has embarked on a mission to satisfy its 'instinctive sense of superiority'…," announced Iran's President Mohamad Khatami at the NAM summit. He also spoke about the "fanatical fundamentalism" of the sole superpower's project to make its own moral and cultural values into eternal and ever-lasting truths.

Even the Indonesian President Megawati Sukarnoputri decided to join the critics of the US administration: "No matter how powerful the country is, that does not give it the right to act unilaterally against another."

"When seen from Asia, the looming war against Iraq appears to have all the hallmarks of an Anglo-Saxon adventure," wrote influential Sri Lankan journalist Marwaan Macan-Markar in his article for the IPS.

Many Asians feel that it is not just the UN that Bush threatens to make irrelevant. It is the entire world that is not white, the entire world that strives to remain culturally different and opposes the world order and one-way globalization.

While the Western media concentrates its attention on the details and minor disagreements between the US and its European allies, men and women in all major Asian cities try to grasp the essence of the issue, asking questions such as: Why doesn't NATO have to disarm if Iraq and other countries do? Why does the US insist on going to war if the great majority of people all over the world oppose such aggression?

Asia suffered tremendously from Western terror. British colonial rulers didn't hesitate to use chemical weapons and extermination techniques against the people of the Middle East (Blair never mentions this when he muses about the "civilized world"). The French ruled brutally over entire Indochina, and the Dutch over Indonesia. And so on!

East Timor lost more than one third of its population during the Indonesian occupation which received a green light from the US and Australia (and was subsequently fueled by the British military industry).

The whole of South Asia and large areas of the Middle East and Far East experienced the "civilized" whip and greed of the British Empire. The Iraqi people suffered from the coup led by Saddam Hussein, supported by the CIA. Iran lost around one million people after it had been invaded by Iraq, armed simultaneously by the US and the USSR.

The US managed to kill millions of innocent people in Indochina, bombing the Cambodian countryside, supporting corrupt and brutal dictatorships in both Southern Vietnam and Cambodia (paving the way for the Khmer Rouge to take power). It carpet-bombed the poor people of isolated Laos. It butchered between one and three million Vietnamese men, women and children, not even caring to find out how many really died – it hardly considered them to be human, anyway.

Cambodian, Laotian and Vietnamese people, and particularly children, are still losing their limbs and lives in the countryside where multitudes of unexploded "bombies" rest at the bottom of rice fields and elsewhere. The US doesn't even bother to cooperate with de-mining agencies.

And on the cultured and civilized front...? What little is left after the intense American bombing of the magnificent towers of the My Son Sanctuary, the spiritual heart of the ancient Champa Kingdom and a UNESCO World Heritage Site, remains a minefield. The great citadel of Imperial Hue, the ancient capital of Vietnam and another UNESCO Heritage site, is still largely a ruin after a devastating US bombardment.

Why on earth should the Asians trust us? Why should they believe that we have a mandate to police the world? We dropped two nukes, they didn't. We had been invading them for centuries, building our glorious "civilized" cities from the theft of their natural resources and the slave labor of their men, women and children. We carpet-bombed them, utilizing all possible weapons of mass destruction, including the notorious 'Agent Orange' that is still poisoning the earth of Indochina.

For millions of Asians whose relatives died, whose economies were ruined and whose entire land areas were reduced to pre-industrial devastation, our past and present involvements are just one terrible reality. It's not like the 'reality' of those who are discussing foreign policy in Parisian cafes, in the wine bars of New York or in the clubs of London. For Asians, it's real reality, it stinks, it makes them shiver in the winter and suffer from horrendous illnesses. It's a reality that leaves millions of people still hungry – people in countries that we tried to "liberate," to "civilize," to make "safe."

And we still sit on our nukes, we still cling to our veto powers, we still push our economic system, our culture and our system of government down the throat of the entire remainder of the world.

The truth is, the rest of the world doesn't like it. And they don't like us. They've had enough of our colonialism, neo-colonialism, arrogance, and wars. They've had enough of our WTOs, IMFs, and World Banks. And it's billions of them, and that's only in Asia.

The CIA, instead of chasing Muslim extremists all over the world, should send their spies to small villages and towns in counties like Indonesia and listen to the voices of the people there. Then they should report back to their masters: report the truth that most Asians are absolutely tired of our hegemony on power. They are restless and ready to act.

It never made it into any newspaper in the West, but after the brutal terrorist attacks on September 11, Vietnamese villagers were firing homemade rockets celebrating the attacks that Vietnamese government (quite correctly) denounced with all its force. Shocking? But remember that they lost millions of people, and nobody even told them: "sorry guys, excuse us, we were wrong. Maybe we should at least give some medical help to your children that we maimed or poisoned." Behaving as we do, we can hardly expect much love and sympathy in this part of the world.

With all the terror and suffering (past and present) that we caused, the only way we can create real peace and stability is to stop, to apologize, and to start working with Asian (and of course, Latin American and African) countries on an equal footing. And, of course, to pay our dues and help to clean up the mess that we created.

Then, and only then, there is a chance that we can be truly supported, appreciated, liked and respected. And above all, forgiven. Instead, Bush and Blair are pushing Asia and the entire planet toward a catastrophe.

Instead of forcing other countries to disarm, we should disarm ourselves. No local dictator managed to bring so much grief on this planet as we did – as our Western civilization did. Let's disarm and then let's (politely) ask others to do the same.

And let's listen to the others, to the majority of people in this world, in all the different parts of the world, instead of applauding the hardly coherent mumblings that are coming from the governments in Paris and Berlin – they have the same goals, but want to use different means. And the reason they are asking for "more time" is because they are still a bit more afraid of their own people than they are of Bush and his entourage.

We are not the chosen people and our truth is not the only truth. There are only two groups that should be allowed to disarm the Iraqi President: one group consists of the Iraqi people themselves. Another group is called 'the people of the world' – the majority of the countries of the General Assembly of the UN. The same majority should also have a right to tell us – the West – to disarm as well as to tell us to comply with the UN resolutions.

Yes, we are all laughing now. We all know that such a suggestion is naïve and absurd. But our laughter may not last too long. It is enough to listen to the words of Malaysian Prime Minister (and each and every journalist working in this part of the world will confirm his words) to have chills running down our spines:

> Our people are getting restless. They want us to do something. If we don't, they will, and they will go against us. Unable to mount a conventional war, they will resort to guerrilla warfare, terrorism against us.

March 2003

The New, Deadly Beginning Of History

Francis Fukuyama was wrong: history didn't end with the collapse of the Soviet Union. The world is at war again and this time the war is not 'cold' at all – it is extremely 'hot'. This war brings a rough awakening for those who hoped that there would be a long, cozy period marked by our world order – a period of peaceful economic dictatorship imposed by the handful of rich and mainly Western states and their multinational companies.

Such global arrangements proved to be simply not good enough for our political leaders and their backers in the corporate world. They obviously felt they have to make a point, to show to the rest of the world who 'is really in charge', to leave no doubts.

Even if we accept that history ended more than a decade ago (just for the sake of argument, since almost nobody really believes that it did) we have to admit that it is starting again, right now, at full speed. If stripped to basics, Fukuyama's theory is based on the doubtful thesis that the end of the history comes when the polarization of the world, 'us' and the Soviets, ends. It comes with the end of the conflict.

There is no Soviet Union anymore, but the world is as polarized as ever. It is still 'us' against 'them', but now 'them' includes almost the entire world, from Latin America to Africa, from Southeast Asia to the Middle East. 'Them' even includes the majority of American people and the overwhelming majority of the citizens of Europe.

This polarization is as dangerous for everyone as it is deadly for global democracy. We convinced the great majority of the world that it has become 'irrelevant'; we spat on the rules of the United Nations. We tried to buy or blackmail foreign governments into submission and into supporting our expansionism. We proved that we don't care what the rest of the world thinks, since we are the biggest bully on the block, that we are 'more equal than the others', that our interests are above anything in the world.

And now we are alone. Governments of the countries that are willing to support our invasion of Iraq (isn't it ironic that the UK and Spain are two of the most brutal colonial powers in human history?) are doing so strictly against the will of their own citizens, yet again re-defining the word 'democracy', a term that is quickly becoming just another cliché.

It seems that we don't care about our isolation, about our unpopularity. Or at least our government doesn't. We don't care that, in a few days and weeks, the whole world will be watching their television screens to see how we will be killing tens, maybe hundreds of thousands, of innocent people in order to satisfy our global dictatorial aspirations.

Most foreign governments will still be cordial toward us. They can't afford not to be – we are too big and too strong and, if they insult us, we may single their countries out and declare them our enemies, terrorists, rogue states. It's fear, a survival instinct, not real, full-hearted support. And submission through fear is what Bush and his administration really wants. As long as we can rule and be obeyed, we don't need to be loved and admired.

While our previous history of the polarized world has been brutal and unsettling (who could ever forget our acts of terror against Vietnam, Laos, Cambodia, Grenada, Panama, Chile, Nicaragua and Cuba to mention just a few places), the emerging chapter of history may be devastating.

If we don't stop now, or if we are not stopped by the rest of the world, our ruling elites may really start to believe that we have been chosen by God to enlighten and save the universe by sword. They will not be the first in the long history of the tyrants ruling enormous and brutal empires.

As a result of this war, we may harvest a tempest. The impoverished world can be expected to revolt and it may do it in an uncontrollable, brutal manner. This revolt would probably be fragmented, uncoordinated and could reduce entire continents to chaos. In such an event, millions of people might lose their lives, hundreds of millions might become hungry and desperate. Saudi Arabia is one of the best candidates for such a scenario, Indonesia, the fourth most populous nation on earth, is another.

The only possible way to stop this madness is to immediately inform the American public about the sentiments or the rest of the world. It is an extremely difficult task, since the interests of big business and the elites control the media. But there may be no other way: the great majority of the American public doesn't realize the gravity of the present situation, for it is not being informed about the fears and grievances of men and women in faraway nations. It doesn't know to what disaster Bush and his backers have been pushing the planet.

If there is anything that can stop the world from our terror, it is the American public itself. Our citizens are not any better or any worst that the citizens of other countries. They possess a natural sense of fair play and, if informed correctly about the situation, most of them will not be willing to support our expansionism. Most of them didn't vote for this president, anyway. Most of them are still against the war!

Public outcry may not stop this war. Nothing can, anymore. But it can prevent many future horrors.

So history is back. We won over the Soviet Union (we starved it through the arms race, to be exact) and we will most definitely win over Iraq, again. We tried to starve Iraq, too, but starvation didn't prove to be a sufficient tool to force its leaders from power. Now we will bomb the Iraqi people back to the Stone Age, in order to get our hands on their natural resources.

But this may be our last major victory. There will be no further support anywhere in the world for our expansionism. Our mafia techniques may mobilize and unite the planet against us. People are afraid only when divided. The last meeting of non-allied nations showed an unprecedented unity of almost all the poor and developing nations (read: the great majority of the world) in their opposition to our hegemony.

Our sixty years of world leadership has proved devastating to almost all continents except Europe. Its cost can be counted in millions of innocent human lives. We should not be allowed to continue. We should be disarmed and forced to rejoin the world community as a nation equal to any other nation on earth, with the same rights and responsibilities, with no nuclear, chemical or biological weapons (we have proved that we cannot be trusted with their possession), a nation respectful of UN resolutions and international treaties.

Let's hope that the human lives that are being lost in Iraq right now will be the last casualties of our complexes of superiority, of our belief that we have a right to sacrifice any number of human beings abroad for our own interests, of the certainty that we are unique and the wisest. And let's hope that, one day, there will be an enormous monument to all those victims of our brutal, merciless imperial past, and that Francis Fukuyama's 'end of history' will become a reality.

March 2003

Cowardly War

Can any country on earth withstand continuous aerial bombardment? Can even the most determined army fight to protect its homeland after having its soldiers, tanks and artillery assailed by tens of thousands of 'precision' bombs, cluster bombs, missiles and heavy artillery shells?

The answer emerging from the burning ashes of Iraqi cities and villages is that there is no way that any defensive war can be fought against the overwhelming superiority of the US air forces.

There are some extremely distorted messages coming from this invasion, similar to those sent many decades ago from the capitals of the former colonial powers.

In the past, European powers plundered and exploited conquered lands. They enslaved their populations, robbing them of freedom, culture, and even of languages and religions in many cases. When the pressure from advancing liberation forces became irresistible, they made concessions: "Now you are free. Now you can govern yourself. We will not pay reparations, we will not even apologize. Now you can compete with us economically, as long as you play by our rules, as long as you put our interests before the interests of your own people, as long as you don't send too many of your people to our prosperous countries."

In today's war, we invaded a foreign country. We 'secured' part of its natural resources, showered tons of high explosives on its cities, and blasted its military forces from the air for more than two weeks. We made sure that no Iraqi aircraft could fly, that no large enemy military unit could move against our forces without being annihilated by an onslaught of ordnance. We bombed Iraq's telecommunications centers, television studios and radio stations. We killed journalists, theirs and ours.

And then we said: "Now you can fight. But make sure that you fight by the rules, by our rules. Make sure that you use weapons that we allow you to use, make sure that you use a strategy and tactics that we consider proper. Do it our way, or else…"

Despite all this, we failed. We dropped hundreds of thousands of propaganda leaflets on Iraqi cities. We told them not to fight, but they chose to disobey us. The people of Iraq don't see us as liberators. Their unwillingness to meekly comply means they are suffering, they are bleeding, and they are burying their dead. The UN claims that, even at this early stage, some 500 thousand Iraqi children are likely to need some psychological counseling after our bombing campaign. The Iraqis hate us, as the Russians hated the Germans, as the Iranians hated the Iraqis, as the Palestinians hate the Israelis. If their defenses weren't being destroyed from the air, every major Iraqi city would become another Stalingrad.

After destroying their defenses from the air and after moving almost unopposed to Baghdad, we claimed the victory. We did it cautiously and without really pronouncing the "V" word. As jubilant crowds flooded some parts of the Iraqi capital, thousands went on a looting rampage. Our armed forces stood by, content.

Using our enormous propaganda machine, we succeeded in inserting some twisted logic into our military campaign. Press conferences in Washington D.C. and Doha overflow with a cheap sentimentality that attempts to cover our brutality and disguise our real goals in the Middle East. "We are not fighting the Iraqi people. We are determined to avoid civilian casualties. We don't want to bomb civilian targets, but because Saddam is such a bastard, sometimes we can't avoid it."

The message that we are invaders and occupiers has got lost, somehow. Over 70 percent of American people now support this war. The promise of active, overwhelming resistance to the war promised by prominent European figures never really materialized – now, the closer our forces approach Baghdad, the softer become the murmurs of criticism from Berlin and Moscow.

Old colonialist and post-colonialist buddies are sometimes critical of our 'unilateral approach', but they will never really cross our path, will never defend our victims, and we know it. We know it with a certainty based upon such examples as

Indochina and Latin America, where we had a free hand to perform whatever barbarity we wished.

The countries that are now openly supporting us are almost exclusively rich. In Asia, only the richest club members stand firmly on our side – Kuwait, Japan, Singapore and South Korea (although even there, public opinion is firmly against the war). The countries of Eastern Europe are not yet rich, but hope to soon become so – too tired of being ruled by outsiders, they now, quite cynically, want to join the oppressors.

The nations of the Middle East are too scared to stand against us. This is, after all, a very good lesson for anyone who dreams of challenging us and our plans.

We, the US and Britain, are now almost alone, hated by most men and women all over the world. But we are not only hated, we are also feared, and that seems to be the goal of our rulers. As long as there is fear, America can continue to rule the world. Britain lost its might after World War II, but now sees an opportunity to become strong again, this time by association.

Iraq is also alone. While billions of people world-wide watch images of this war in fascinated horror and express their sympathy for its victims, almost nobody dares to come to the rescue of a country that has been singled out as an enemy of the mightiest colonial empire on earth.

Talk about the rationale behind this conflict has also melted away. When Scott Ritter[5] claims that Iraq has no nuclear weapons and probably no chemical nor biological weapons, the sycophantic media in the West pays no attention to him, nor to anyone else daring to challenge the morality of this invasion.

Instead, direct and indirect censorship in the United States is becoming blatant, a warning of the realities of the brave new world that is probably waiting for us somewhere down the road.

Anger is brewing in the Middle East, in Indonesia, the Philippines, Malaysia, Africa and Latin America. "It's not a war against Islam, it's a war against humanity," declared the government of Indonesia. Cairo is warning that there may be a hundred bin-Ladens if the war continues. Hundreds of international experts are warning that the war may expand.

But maybe that's what we want! War is good for defense contractors and companies that produce the weapons. It's also good for those who want to force the rest of the world into submission. During a war it's easy to control the domestic press and public dissent. And many at home are grateful for it, anyway, for it offers free, continuous entertainment for no extra cost.

---

[5] Former lead inspector for UNSCOM's Concealment and Investigations until he resigned in late 1998, a former US Marine intelligence officer, and a Republican. His recent book, written with William Rivers Pitt, is called *War On Iraq: What Team Bush Doesn't Want You to Know*, Profile Books, 2002.

Despite our recent 'push' toward Baghdad, there is no doubt that this is a cowardly war. Everyone is consumed by fear. Our military planners were afraid to confront the Iraqi soldiers instead of bombing them (and civilians) from the air. The Bush administration is scared of losing control of the world, and is therefore constantly discovering new enemies. Our media tycoons are afraid of the truth, and many of the people sitting in front of their television sets in the United States are afraid of opening their eyes.

They are scared to accept that the jubilant crowd in Baghdad is not really welcoming us – it is celebrating the departure of a regime that we helped to arm when we needed it to invade Iran. We are not being greeted as liberators anymore. The glorious days of the beaches of Normandy are over. In desperate and humiliated nations all over the world, our flags and guns no longer evoke thoughts about freedom and democracy. They evoke fear. They fuel resentment. Most of all, they fan the flames of a burning desire to fight for a just and peaceful world, against our hegemony.

April 2003

Castro's Loneliness in Asia

The Western media happily commented on the Asian trip of the Cuban leader, Fidel Castro. The International Herald Tribune, for example, spoke of the awkward friendship between Cuba and two Asian Communist states – China and Vietnam – under the title: "Castro in China: 'How you've changed'."

The bottom lines of all the reports were almost identical: While China and Vietnam are unstoppably marching toward the glory of the market economy, Cuba is stuck with an ideology that nobody (except North Korea, maybe) cherishes.

When Castro arrived in Hanoi, the main arteries of the city were, as usual, decorated with red hammers and sickles. The streets of the Vietnamese capital were congested with hundreds of thousands of motorbikes and lined with a chaotic medley of innumerable private shops and services.

People came to welcome Fidel. They came to the airport and to the square in front of the Ho Chi Minh mausoleum, but these were not spontaneous gatherings. The entire visit had been pre-arranged – Castro didn't even have a chance to deliver one of his famous hours-long speeches. Unless one had been invited by the government, there was no way to get close to the legendary Cuban leader who, decades ago, during the 'American War' came to Hanoi and declared that the Cuban people were ready to shed their blood for Vietnam.

Castro visited old Vietnamese generals, held talks with the government and the Party officials, received a promise of Vietnamese rice and discussed options to increase trade between two countries. He went to a performance, attended only by high-ranking officials and diplomats, at the Hanoi Opera. There were smiles and embraces, handshakes and compliments. But what country had the Cuban leader visited? Was it really a Communist state for which the Cuban people had been ready to fight and die?

The answer is, of course, 'No'. Although the media in the West likes to call Vietnam 'communist', along with other 'remaining communist states', such as Laos, Cuba, China and North Korea, Vietnam has lately become an extremely strange hybrid of Confucianism and wild capitalism, with some leftover Marxist slogans.

The Vietnam Communist Party still officially rules the country, but the state owns less than 70 percent of the country's GDP. Some enterprises are controlled by corrupt officials and run almost like private companies.

There is no guarantee of free medical care and free education as had always been the case in all countries of the former Soviet block. Shelter is not guaranteed. Vietnamese citizens have to pay for medical treatment: surgery, or any serious illness, may wipe out family savings. Some patients at the state hospitals have to sell their houses or apartments in order to pay for medical bills. Almost nobody has medical insurance. Basic education is compulsory but not free.

Misery is widespread. Decades after the war, Vietnam remains one of the poorest countries in the world, with the annual GDP per capita of 480 dollars. Minimal wages (just increased) are around 18 dollars a month. These numbers wouldn't mean much if Vietnam was a 'social state'. It isn't.

The distribution of wealth in Vietnam is worse than in some 'capitalist' countries such as Thailand and Malaysia and, on paper at least, even worse than in India. There is almost nothing 'social' or 'socialist' about Vietnam, even nothing that could be associated with the failed and perverted attempts of the Soviet Union to create a workers paradise.

There is no public transportation in major Vietnamese cities, except a few bus routes. Even in Ho Chi Minh City and Hanoi, 'mass transit' is utilized by well under ten percent of the population. There are no state stores (they used to be often half-empty in Russia and still are in Cuba, but at least they used to have some basic food for rock bottom prices, affordable even for the poorest segments of the society). There are almost no food subsidies. Prices for milk, yogurt and fruits, essential for children's diets, are financially out of reach for the majority of the population.

To be rich is in vogue. In a recent article in "Vietnam Economic Review" it was reported that children of party officials often burn one hundred dollar bills in the new nightclubs and discotheques, just to show how far away they are from the mainstream Vietnamese.

While the citizens have to pay for their medical treatment and for the education of their children, new government buildings are growing in expensive areas of the capital. Brand new SUVs and limousines with official and military license plates are pushing their way through the sea of motorbikes on Hanoi's streets.

Vietnam is a country that is visited every year by eager students from prestigious American universities. Obviously, many in the West see Vietnam as an extremely sound economic model: an increasingly open economy (so what if there is screaming corruption) and almost non-existent social spending!

Cuba and Vietnam have nothing in common.

During my last visit to Havana, I was invited to the apartment of one of the members of the Central Committee. He was over 60 years old and ill. But every morning he went to work on a bicycle – "My people are suffering and I am not going to waste state money on the car and gas." His apartment had only one bedroom and no elevator. His television was still black and white.

Even after the collapse of the Soviet bloc, dirt-poor Cuba managed to provide excellent free medical care, vaccinations, free education and rationed, but almost free, food. Right now it has the longest life expectancy of any

Latin American country, almost equal to that of the United States, as well as the best-educated population.

While Cuban intellectuals and artists, writers, musicians, dancers and filmmakers excel all over the world: Vietnam's cultural export is close to zero. Cuba is international and internationalist: Vietnam is closed, dwelling on its 'cultural preservation'. The Cubans are obsessed with books and films from all over the globe. Havana hosts one of the best film festivals in the world, whereas Hanoi, with two million inhabitants, has only three small cinemas, and almost no famous artists from abroad are allowed to perform there.

Cubans are passionate about politics. Political issues are discussed day and night at home, in cafes or in hole-in-the-wall local pubs over the rum and the smoke from black tobacco. Vietnamese seem to be indifferent to politics. Revolution is not a passion, just some cliche that no one takes seriously anymore.

In Hanoi, Ms. Ha, my Vietnamese friend, explained to me that the Vietnamese revolution was supposed to unite the country, not to create a social state.

In Havana, revolution is still a passion. People love it or hate it, but there is no indifference. They write songs about it, and they write books and poems. They are willing to starve for it if they are true 'revolutionaries' or are willing to risk their lives to escape from the island if they are against it.

Hanoi is a pragmatic and business oriented place. Solidarity exists inside the families but not on the street, not in the country as a whole. Idealism is almost non-existent: longing for financial success rules the lives of many privileged citizens of the capital. Those who are poor, the great majority in Hanoi or in the countryside, seem to have no more hopes or dreams left, but are resigned to live their subsistence lives on a bare minimum, without counting on any substantial help or social justice.

There seems to be no joy on the streets of Hanoi. The city is colorful and some of its districts are attractive. But one doesn't hear laughter. Everyone seems to be concerned with his or her own life. Everyone seems to look straight ahead, unconcerned with the others, unconcerned with the city, or the entire world. Revolution ended! Or it was postponed? Or did it never really happen?

Fidel left. He is back on his green island that still evokes passion in millions of people all over the planet. He is loved and he is hated. He is admired and condemned. But everyone knows his name, no matter where! He is proud and his people are proud. They may be poor, but they feed the hungry, they help the sick and they educate their children.

When still under the colonial boot, the Africans learned to count on Cuban soldiers who fought and died for their freedom. Desperate nations all over the world gratefully accepted Cuban doctors and teachers, as well as Cuban vaccines.

The International Herald Tribune was wrong. Cuba is not 'one of the Communist countries'. It stands alone. It gave when it was able to give and, with the great exception of China, received nothing when it was itself in need. Cuba is our bad conscience and our pride. Nevertheless, for many of us it is, and will always be, a reminder that there are still men and women on this planet who are not willing to sell their beliefs for some new motorbike or a shiny mobile phone.

Cuban people believe in equality (even some of their dissidents do); they believe in social justice. They sing songs about it and they dance in order to support each other in moments when the world around them seems too scary and threatening. The banners and stars are for real there, not just for the illumination of the main avenues. And when they shout "Socialismo o muerte, carajo!" (Socialism or death, damn it!), it sounds real and it is real, for many of them at least, and probably for the majority.

April 2003

War Against The War

by Andre Vltchek and William Toth

"These are very patriotic times," explains Jack, a middle aged man who is wearing a war veteran's hat. "We have many boys in the troops now. West Virginia provides more soldiers for the army than any other state of the union. I am a war veteran myself, so you will hear nothing negative about our troops here."

Jack thinks for a while, tries to formulate his own ideas, then he continues: "On the other hand, there are some contradictions about our involvement in Iraq. Some people think – who are we to stick our nose in their business."

It's early afternoon, Saturday, in one of the poorest towns of West Virginia that is in turn the poorest state of the United States of America. Once a thriving coal-mining town, today War is a dirty and haggard community of mainly retired or unemployed people.

Decay is most evident on Legion Street, the two-mile thoroughfare that serves as the last lifeline of this town. Buildings that once proudly defined the city center are now coal dust gray and broken, some with missing windows and plywood hammered over what is left of the entrance doors.

Passenger trains don't stop at War, anymore. The train station has been converted to a small, but functional, city hall and community center. A building not even the size of a gas station is now the city government. Now, only heavy cargoes pulled by two powerful locomotives shake the ground of the center of sleepy War.

"Brewster's Drive-In," a kiosk that serves coffee and sandwiches with three outdoor tables, has become a social center of the town. This is where old men and women come in their old pick-up trucks, or on foot, so they can meet their neighbors. It's where people come to discuss the almost non-existent work prospects, war and peace, unemployment benefits....

Mr. Jones grew up in this town before the Second World War. He is also a war veteran, having fought the Japanese in Mindanao, Philippines. He is dressed in a loud yellow t-shirt. He has a remnant flat top hair style and several of his teeth are missing, but he doesn't mind, offering to anyone who is willing to listen an endless supply of wise cracks: "You are asking me how this town has changed in the last 60 years? Well, let's start by saying that during that time there have been no improvements whatsoever! Now, this is really a free society: everybody is either unemployed or lives on welfare."

"In the past, War had three car dealers and two movie theaters. On Saturday nights our streets used to be so busy; people were strolling until midnight. Most of the stores had to be open at least until eleven. There was either a bus or train leaving from the center every 10 to 15 minutes. We used to have 3 hospitals. Look, there used to be a funeral home, and this ruin – it used to be a hotel. Over there was a gas station. Now we have nothing. There are 20 thousand people living in this county but we don't have one movie theater or a car dealer. There used to be 3 hospitals in the county, now we have only one."

"So you want to know what I think about the war with Iraq?" suddenly his face becomes serious. "Honestly I think it was a mistake to go there; a mistake and a waste of money. I don't think it was the right thing to do. They haven't proven that Iraq has any weapons of mass destruction."

"We have a history of going where we are not supposed to be," he continues. "I remember that when the war with Japan began, everybody was glued to the radios. We were all imagining Japanese landing on our beaches. My best friend volunteered, joined the army right after Pearl Harbor. But even then I kept telling the people: 'why should we go there? What were we doing there to begin with? Pearl Harbor is 100 million miles away! What's the point of going to war so far away from home?"

One conversation led to another and people began to gather around us at the kiosk. Nearly all men there are former marines. Jack was right; men of West Virginia are considered to be good with weapons. Many of them were, or are hunters. They are always drafted in disproportional numbers. But being former marines from West Virginia doesn't automatically translate to the support of the current day military adventures.

All the men too have spent time serving underground, in the coal mines. Skeet, a senior with a quick smile and a hearty handshake came thundering up on a converted police motorcycle. It was his pride and joy. He is a war and a coal mine veteran and knowing the history of both, we were happy to be talking with him that day. His father, along with 90 other miners died in a coal mine explosion some 30 years earlier. "The mines are safer now, but coal is running out in War."

Debbie, an African-American lady in her 30s arrives at Brewster's Drive- In with her young daughter. "I didn't support the war but I felt that I had no choice but to support the troops. But I don't believe that we should have gotten involved there – in Iraq – in a first place. We have so many problems back home and nobody takes care of them. I hated all that killing of the innocent people. And anyway, our politicians didn't accomplish what they went there for."

Once asked if there were any organized protests, Debbie smiles, almost ironically: "No, there were no organized protests and no gatherings or discussions. At school they told my daughter: 'there is going to be a war...' as if there were no doubts."

Unemployment in War stands at 69 percent; the majority of the county workforce is idle. The biggest employer in War is the Board of Education; still American flags decorate every structure in the center of the city.

War mainly supports the Democratic Party, but on some issues it is extremely conservative. "Bush won in West Virginia," explains one of the visitors of Brewster's Drive-In. "He won because he was for guns and West Virginia is strictly for guns."

In a small privately run Museum in Hatfield, WV, Jane Hatfield (Granddaughter of William Anderson – Devil Anse Hatfield of the famous Hatfield and McCoy feud) a Republican and a chain smoker, explains that while there are 20 Democrats to every Republican in the county, many supported the invasion of Iraq after it started, feeling obliged to "back our boys."

She said, "Almost everybody had some doubts about the administration's motives, but there were few public discussions, even in the churches. While we talked with her, a sad looking couple dropped in to buy a headstone for the grave of a child, underlining the desperation of these times for these people.

Back at the kiosk, people come and go, and some are determined to stay for hours. Even two out of town reporters like us can provide welcome entertainment, an escape from the monotony of the day-to-day life.

It seems like almost nobody in War supported the American invasion of Iraq. But then, nobody protested against it, either. There were no anti-French sentiments here, no desires to make United Nations "irrelevant," no "you are with us or against us" attitude.

It is therefore safe to conclude that the citizens of one of the poorest community in the United States were passively opposed to foreign invasion, while voting for Bush in the last elections.

I asked Jack if the people of War knew anything about Iraq. "Yes, he answered, we watch CNN quite a bit. And we have some people from the East like Italians, Germans, Polish and stuff. Some have even ties with their old countries."

"At least they told children something about Iraq," said Debbie. "At school, they told them where it is and something about the history."

Declining friendly invitations to stay and share music and more fellowship with the people of War, we decided to hit the road, having some 350 miles ahead of us. There was something surreal about this visit, something peculiar about people we left behind.

Here were some of the poorest people in America who voted for a Republican President just because he supports gun ownership. These people were essentially skeptical about the motives of the US foreign invasions in the far away places, sometimes even hostile to them, yet almost every middle aged man we talked to was a war veteran. It seemed that the more crumbling, the more destroyed the street, the more flags and patriotic slogans it accommodated.

The country has lately been a place of surreal contradictions. Its poorest towns, including War, West Virginia, are obviously no exceptions to the general confusion.

June 2003

"Activist Nuns" From Tennessee

by Andre Vltchek and William Toth

Sister Anne Hablas is a fragile looking lady, over 70 years of age. She is alert, quick and knowledgeable on wide range of domestic and international issues. She has a Master's degree in history. She is a nun – a nun who doesn't hesitate to challenge the authorities even after the beginning of the witch hunt that began against political activists in the US after September 11th.

She believes in social justice, and she is a pacifist (although without openly denying the right of those in Latin America or anywhere else to use force while fighting against our expansionism). She is a member of several grassroots, community based organizations. She is currently working with the Catholic Diocese of Knoxville in the Office of Justice-Peace-Integrity of Creation.

Anne Hablas believes that the production of nuclear weapons is (and always has been) wrong, that the bombing of two Japanese cities – Hiroshima and Nagasaki – at the end of the war was nothing but barbaric. She insists that the production of nuclear weapons in the United States should stop immediately. Exactly that (especially actions based on her beliefs) is what leads her in the direction of repeated collisions with the law.

Sister Anne, an associate Sister Mary (presently on probation after serving part of her term in prison), and other nuns do over and over again what even strong, young and healthy men don't dare to do anymore. They walk toward the restricted area on the road serving the "Y-12" plant in Oak Ridge, Tennessee (historically a uranium enrichment facility, responsible for the production of bombs that were dropped on Hiroshima and Nagasaki). In defiance of the regulations and laws they cross the demarcation line marching toward the plant.

The reaction is without exception extreme. The nuns are intercepted and arrested by the local city police, thrown in jail, tried, sentenced by the jury and in many cases, forced to serve prison terms.

But for them, it is a part of the struggle. On April 9, 2003, Anne Hablas read her Court Statement for trial in Anderson County Courthouse, turning it into a powerful political statement:

> My name is Anne Hablas. For 50 years I have been a member of the Presentation Sisters of Fargo, North Dakota, a Catholic Order of Nuns.... I am a long-time member of the Oak Ridge

Environmental Peace Alliance and believe that the production of nuclear weapons at the Y-12 Plant in Oak Ridge is a violation of Article VI of the Nuclear Non-proliferation Treaty which was signed by the United States in 1970. Furthermore, by not observing the requirements of this Treaty which was ratified by the United States Senate and promulgated as law, the United States is violating the U.S. Constitution, Article VI, which declares that all treaties "made...under the Authority of the United States, shall be the supreme Law of the Land; and the Judges in every State shall be bound thereby..."

I was brought up to believe that the law is to be respected and obeyed, but I was also made aware that by my Baptism as a Catholic I am ultimately called to follow my conscience. A letter I received when I was discerning whether I would do civil disobedience at Y-12 on March 30 helped me to make the choice I did. This letter referred to Franz Jagerstatter, an Austrian peasant, who because of his refusal to serve in Hitler's army was imprisoned and eventually executed by the German government in 1943. Franz withstood hostility and accusations of being unpatriotic and a traitor, but he believed he had to obey his conscience.

He was subsequently vindicated by the judges of the Nuremberg War Crime Tribunal in 1950 who wrote: "Individuals have international duties which transcend the national obligations of obedience.... Therefore individual citizens have the duty to

> violate domestic laws to prevent crimes against peace and humanity from occurring."
>
> I accept responsibility for my actions, and whether I am judged guilty or innocent, I was acting in accord with a Higher Law to which I must be faithful.

The Jury found Anne Hablas guilty of the ridiculous crime that she was arrested for: obstructing traffic on the public roadway. She spent two nights in jail and was released. [These reporters visited the site of arrest and were convinced that no obstruction of traffic took place].

Obvious to any person traveling on the public road is the fact that (taking into account Sr. Anne's description) no criminal trespass was committed. It was impossible because the demarcation line was guarded by temporary iron gates. These facts were shown in photographs documenting the day.

Sister Anne seems to be indifferent toward what happened to her personally, but she is passionate about the fate of the other "comrades in arms":

> I was not the only one who crossed the blue line. It was six of us, including Judy Ross, an 80 year old lady who ended up spending 1 month in jail for 'disobeying police officer'. Last year, sister Mary was tried by the jury and by Federal Judge for crossing the 'blue line'. Her trial lasted 4 days.
>
> As a pattern, judges don't allow any arguments about the US violating international laws or

treaties or about the morality of producing nuclear weapons. Judges simply don't allow this kind of discussion. And it seems that the guilty verdict is a norm. Judy was sentenced to 2 months in prison while Mary had to serve time in the Federal facility in Kentucky. Mary openly declared that she is a prisoner of conscience.

Anne Hablas claims that most Americans have no idea how many political prisoners we hold in our jails:

3 sisters went to protest at the testing site in Colorado and now they are facing many years in jail. They are held in terrible conditions, in high security jail. They are waiting for the sentencing, but they have already spent months in these conditions.

The US government is introducing new dangerous laws and regulations. There is a witch-hunt on people of non-white color of skin, especially if they have Middle Eastern origin. Now even the libraries have to produce records about people if the FBI asks them. If the agent asks what somebody had been reading, the librarian has to produce records, without informing the person in question.

According to her and to her friends, America is undergoing a period of profound militarization. The entire US leadership, including the President and members of Congress are people who came from the corporate establishment and are getting millions of dollars from the corporations. The country is run according to corporate interests, not according to the needs of the majority of the people.

"So I fear for my country," Anne Hablas admits. "The Iraq war brought many people to action, even here in Knoxville, which can be described as a conservative town. On the other hand, the Catholic Church is mostly silent. Even during the sermon, if a priest dares to condemn the war, there is someone who is ready to interrupt him: 'what does this have to do with the mass?' And people clap. So sometimes we get hopeful but other times very disappointed, especially considering that even the Vatican condemned the war and the production of nuclear weapons but that this message is not often heard and discussed in our churches!"

Therefore Anne Hablas, a senior Catholic nun decided to take action, without waiting for others. In Tennessee, she and her friends are becoming a kind of folk legend. People talk about them, some with respect, others with annoyance. They were once called jokingly "terrorist nuns," but this is only a joke, being as far from the truth as possible, for they are gentle souls doing good work.

"These women are fantastic," says local folk singer and songwriter Nancy Brennan Strange: "And I am going to write a song about them. It will be a song about our "activist nuns."

July 2003

Malaysia and Singapore Revisited

All of you probably had a chance to hear or read it somewhere: Malaysia and Singapore are two dictatorships, two systems that violate basic human rights and limit freedom of speech and of the press. Their leaders stay in power for too long and their ruling political parties go unchallenged in every election.

Sounds bad, doesn't it? The only major problem with this (mainly Western) theory is that the great majority of the citizens of these countries would strongly disagree.

Wee Gee, an owner of a trendy jazz club in Singapore, has his own theory:

> They all come here – Australians, Britons and other Europeans, and they can't stand the place because it destroys their theories about Asia. They like to see underdevelopment because it makes them feel secure and superior. Their favorite places

are Cambodia and Vietnam. After two days in Singapore, they realize that we have probably the best social system in the world, good city planning, clean, safe streets and excellent public transportation. So they think: 'Wow, how did these Chinks and Malays and Indians achieve such a high standard of living? There must be something hiding in the closet. And they start bashing us. Understand, for an average white Australian it is simply psychologically unacceptable that there is an Asian country that is richer than his.

Neighboring Malaysia hardly escapes devastating criticism either. It is bashed in the Western press from the right and from the left, accused of almost feudal governance by some, of introducing affirmative action for the Malay majority by others, for spending too much money on mega-projects (tallest buildings in the world, new capital city, gigantic international airport, the largest Muslim museum in the world, to name just a few) or simply for harshly attacking Western foreign policy and two recent US-led invasions.

Both Singapore and Malaysia are attacked by the Western left for being "too capitalist" and by the right for "not having free, open and transparent economies" (referring to extremely cozy relations between local companies and the government, a model that originally comes from Japan and is known in Malaysia as 'Malaysia Incorporated').

So, what is it really that irks the West about these two countries in Southeast Asia that were nicknamed dragons and tigers and other potent creatures before 1997? Without any doubt, the answer is: their relative success!

Malaysian GDP per head is only 3,920 dollars a year (The Economist: 'The World in 2002'). That's only slightly higher than in Latin American countries such as Brazil and Peru. The difference is that there is almost no extreme poverty left in 'undemocratic' Malaysia, while one would have a hard time trying not to notice the widespread misery in Brazil and Peru, which we consider 'free' and 'democratic' much more readily.

Before the 1997 "economic crisis" (though in fact the 1997 crisis had nothing to do with the economy), Malaysia made incredible progress, mainly due to a well-planned economy, an extremely hard working population, and huge investment in social policies and infrastructure. As was the case in Singapore decades earlier, against all odds Malaysia became a relatively balanced middle class country, transforming itself from a traditional agricultural society into a developed industrial nation. During the crisis, for which international currency speculators were largely to blame, Malaysia lost around forty percent of its wealth overnight, but, unlike neighboring Indonesia, did not plunge into chaos and prevailed.

Today, six years after the beginning of the crisis, Malaysia is again a socially balanced, multi-racial and multi-cultural nation with relatively good medical care, education and infrastructure, called by Joseph Stiglitz a "good example for other developing countries." Although the Western media constantly reports on its 'hidden racial tensions', it is probably one of the most tolerant nations in Asia.

Nearby, Singapore managed to completely eradicate poverty more than a decade ago, creating one of the best (if not the best) social systems in the world that provides not only basics like excellent medical care and education, but also subsidized housing, advanced public transportation and world class cultural institutions including museums and concert halls.

Writing bitterly and defensively, an attitude born out of the 1997 situation, Malaysian Prime Minister Mahathir Mohamad snaps at the West:

> We have tried to defend ourselves as best as we could, but, for some of us, every move we make to revive our economies has been immediately condemned as a ploy to help members of the ruling parties and their cronies. It is impossible for non-Asian foreign detractors to believe that Asian government leaders can be honest at all. If Asian leaders do anything at all for the good of their countries, it must be because they are corrupt and want to help their cronies and their families. Such prejudiced and stereotyped views will, I fear, persist for a long time to come. The people who espouse such views, it must be remembered, are the descendants of the old white-supremacist colonialists. They cannot get rid of their old bugaboos no matter how far their civilizations have supposedly advanced. We simply cannot expect justice and fair play for Asians and Africans; we have had to ignore all the prejudice and get on with rebuilding our economies. (Mahathir Mohamad: "A New Deal For Asia," Pelanduk, 1999).

It is true that Malaysia and Singapore (as well as other developed Asian countries) are facing continuous and vicious attacks from the West. Malaysia is far from perfect, but it can hardly be called a dictatorship.

After the 1997-98 crisis that impoverished millions of Malays while enriching hundreds of foreign speculators, Mahathir declared that the free market system had proved to be a failure and fired his finance minister, Anwar Ibrahim. Mr. Ibrahim was beaten by police, and accused of sodomy and corruption. Almost one year later, he was found guilty and sentenced to six years in prison.

That was enough to trigger an enormous media campaign against Malaysia in general and against its political system in particular. The fate of Anwar Ibrahim attracted more attention from Western analysts and media than did the millions of citizens of Malaysia who had become victims of an inhuman, brutal global economic dictatorship and had seen the fruits of decades of their hard work wiped out overnight.

The opinion of foreigners about Malaysia didn't change much even after Ibrahim's wife, Azizah Ismail, formed a new opposition 'National Justice Party', but gained only five of the 193 seats contested in the November 1999 elections.

So why are Malaysia and Singapore the center of negative attention for people in the West, while there is generally a consensual silence about so many other places on earth where injustice is indisputable? To speak about 'political cronyism' (the highly popular expression for describing Southeast Asian leaders and business elite) one doesn't have to leave the West itself to find examples that would make almost any Southeast Asian nation look like a model of order and civility by comparison. Italy, for example: with its

Fascist and indisputably criminal Prime-Minister Silvio Berlusconi who (just by coincidence?) exercises almost unlimited control over the nation's media.

In the great majority of 'democracies' in the Western Hemisphere, Malaysian economic, social and political standards (not to mention Singaporean standards which at least in the social field are even higher than those in the United States) would be seen as an undeniably high achievement.

One explanation could be that almost all injustices in Latin America are the result of Western (white) colonial rule. While Malaysia and Singapore are governed either by members of the majority or of a substantial minority, most of the people in Latin America are still controlled by a white minority, including in those countries where indigenous people form the majority. Those who dare to challenge this state of affairs are intimidated, marginalized, ridiculed or driven into exile. Even the Nobel Peace Prize Laureate Rigoberta Manchu was forced to leave her native Guatemala after vicious attacks against her (her main fault, it seems, was that she was 'fat, indigenous and a woman') and move to neighboring Mexico.

The distribution of wealth in our Latin American protectorates is the worst in the world, and coherent social policies are almost nonexistent. Freedom of the press is mainly the preserve of those who can afford to print newspapers and magazines. Furthermore, there is almost no serious criticism of Latin American semi-dictatorships by our media.

In comparison to most of the 'third world' countries, Malaysia is a star. Its social model is applicable more or less everywhere, its proud (but pragmatic) refusal to follow European and North American economic and social models can eventually attract followers from all over the world, undermining the Western hegemony of global power in the so called "developing world." For instance, last year in Lima, I was told by Raffo Munoz (First Secretary of the Communist Party of Peru) that he "is studying the Malaysian model very carefully and is extremely interested in finding out how it could be implemented in Peru."

Belief in 'Asian Values' (although this expression itself can be a bit dubious, and those very values can sometimes be compared with old Christian fundamentalist values of the past, as Mahathir himself admits) are putting Malaysia and Singapore in the forefront of the movement for Asian (or at least Asia-Pacific) unity and resistance against foreign domination. The Malaysian government is extremely outspoken when it comes to criticism of the Western invasions and 'world order', our economic and cultural hegemony, our re-emerging habit of disregarding international opinion and our willingness to act openly in (exclusively) our own interests.

Malaysian and Singaporean achievements are based on domestically grown models and at least partially have their roots in local cultures. The main purpose of those models was, and is, an improvement of the lives of Malaysian and Singaporean citizens.

In many Asian countries there is still a popular belief that the 1997 crisis was triggered by the West, in order to prevent the Asian model from truly taking off. Although there is no proof that there was any coordinated, premeditated design to ruin the Malaysian, Indonesian, South Korean and Philippine economies after the collapse of the Thai baht (although the pressure of international advisors and organizations on the then still well-performing Malaysian economy to devalue the ringgit only because of the speculation that 'it will not be able to be competitive after a Thai devaluation of the baht' did enormous harm to start with), it was obvious that the world's institutions and most powerful governments did nothing to stop the insane and unjust economic downward spiral of the late nineties.

Today, Malaysia is again a developing country with first world infrastructure and social systems. Its streets are safe, its hospitals clean and its highways almost as good as those in Germany or France. Its bookstores are well stocked, providing the latest reads from all over the world. There are no homeless people on the streets of Kuala Lumpur, no ghettos for minorities, and no child prostitutes.

There is a death penalty and it is used. For those of us who see the death penalty as something immoral and perverted, this system cannot be viewed as perfect. Sharia law now applies for Muslims in two states controlled by Islamic parties. A woman was recently arrested for "sitting in a bus too close to a man she was not related to." For those of us who write books, Malaysia is a place that should improve in many ways. Of course there is censorship: no books that ridicule the government, challenge religions or "promote Zionism" (read: are sympathetic to Jews). For those of us who believe that one of the basic and undeniable human rights is to have religion or to have no religion at all, the constant emphasis on faith may be something deeply annoying and disturbing. Malaysian 'cooperation with the war on terror' leaves plenty of space for criticism, as does its mishandling of illegal immigrants (mainly after 9-11), in Kalimantan and elsewhere.

The Singaporean government cravenly supported the US invasion of Iraq, despite public opinion against the war (not much different than in Spain, Italy or Japan). It does intimidate opposition and applies the death penalty and other inhuman punishments. Although there is no exact data (and in the recent interview for the BBC, the Singaporean Prime Minister admitted that even he is not familiar with the numbers) it is estimated that Singapore executes over 80 people a year. Adjusted for size, this would equal around 6,500 people that would be executed every year in the United States (the US executed 71 people in 2002)!

But there is no perfect society on this planet. In other societies with less than 4,000 dollars GDP per capita (as in Malaysia), millions of people starve or live in subsistence conditions. They rot in understaffed hospitals with no basic medicine. They live in polluted, overcrowded cities with enormously high crime rates. Malaysian achievements (not to speak about Singapore's) are enormous.

If I had to choose either to live in increasingly orderly and clean Kuala Lumpur or in insanely divided, polluted, poor and anarchic Lima, I, as a writer, would choose Lima with no hesitation. I would always choose chaos over order! However, there are not many writers in the world, and people like me are in minority. The great majority of men and women are scared of misery, they want to have their own house and small car, a good, safe school for their children, clean, attractive streets for walking, and fast trains to get them from point A to point B. These people with families and children who aim at security and a good middle class life wouldn't hesitate one second: they would choose Kuala Lumpur.

We all know that with such a small GDP per capita, countries like Malaysia "shouldn't have all these social privileges." According to our world order, the Malaysians should concentrate on feeding OUR economies, OUR companies, sacrificing their children and their families in the process. One of the reasons why our media people and opinion-making gurus hate Malaysia and Singapore is not only because these countries learned how to say "NO" to us, but also because they are putting the interests of their own people first. That's why we can't forgive them, but at the same time can forgive everything to our Latin American colonies and their white elites who are always happy to sacrifice entire nations for their allegiance to their European/Western blood and culture. We can forgive them their many forms of apartheid as well as the swollen bellies of the starving children in Northern Nicaragua and Southwestern Honduras. We can forgive racial segregation in Peru, Ecuador and Bolivia – former strongholds of great cultures that we managed to destroy! We can forgive Mexican latifundistas and still call Mexico a democracy.

Every inch of progress made in Malaysia and Singapore is another nail in the coffin of Western domination and modern day colonialism. We grieve over their success and celebrate their downfalls.

Malaysia should reform, it should drop censorship, the death penalty, authoritarianism, but it should stay on course when it comes to its social policy. It should keep putting its people first. It should teach other developing countries worldwide how to do the same; how to care about the welfare of their own people, to unite in order to defend culture and principles, to have the guts to say 'no' to the superpower when necessary.

Both Singapore and Malaysia are far from perfect. So are we. But if (in the case of Malaysia) there is no sharp turn toward religious fundamentalism, both countries will be able to offer a sound social alternative as a model to the developing world.

August 2003

East Timor - Indonesian Amnesia

Timor Leste: At 55 she looks shockingly old and frail. She lives in Ermera – a poor town lost in the green lush hills of East Timor – Timor Leste, of the youngest country on earth. Of course she has a name, but it is irrelevant to quote it here – her fate is the same as that of so many women of her land. I follow her with my eyes as she walks slowly to the main street, to the market.

She looks more like a spirit than a living person. I was told that she, as with so many women of this land, had been gang raped by Indonesian soldiers some twenty years ago. As if rape were not enough, she was tortured, burned, humiliated. She survived, unlike so many others. And as with tens of thousands of women of Timor, Leste lost her son and her husband and her house.

After witnessing the horrors of the Indonesian occupation of East Timor several times in the past, after being arrested and tortured myself for simply trying to do my work – to alert the world about the genocide – I decided to return again to Ermera, to the area that witnessed some of the fiercest resistance battles. I came to interview this woman, or some woman like her, to interview any woman that survived the horrors of the occupation. But when I saw her in Ermera, I couldn't approach her, I couldn't ask her to relive her past.

East Timor is free. It is living what can be described as "Year Zero." It is still dirt poor, desperate, confused and in pain. Even combatants of resistance get almost no help from the government. Recently, one of the legendary commanders reduced to the subsistent existence of selling wood, drove to the house of President Gusmao, almost running his guards over, and yelled: "Look at me, this is what I became. Buy my wood." And Gusmao bought it with his own money and just stood there, repeating to his former comrade in arms: "I don't know what to do. I am a President, but what can I do?"

I have been asked by my Indonesian friends: "How is East Timor doing now? With all that foreign aid they are getting, is the situation improving?" This simple and innocent question shocked me. How can the nation that lost over 30 percent of its population recover in two or three years? And then I understood: 'They really don't know. They don't realize the magnitude of the past extermination. They don't realize that the policy of "transmigrasi" ("trans-migration," when those dead were 'replaced' by the Muslims from Java and Sumatra and even Hindus from Bali) was in fact ethnic cleansing on an enormous scale'.

Much bigger Chile lost 3 to 4 thousand people during and after the coup and has still not fully recovered from the shock and nightmares of the military dictatorship. And it is not expected to fully recover anytime soon. If East Timor were the size of Chile, it would have lost proportionally over 5 million people.

"This country is being helped and to a certain extent controlled by the foreigners," explained a student of political science. "We are grateful to them, but they don't understand us. Their job is to make our economy work, to establish our institutions as quickly as possible. But this nation is still in shock, it is still in deep trauma. And people who fought for our freedom – the soil and blood of this country – are now close to starvation. Look at Indonesia. When they won independence against Holland, Sukarno took to his government and to the top military ranks those men who fought for freedom, even if they were illiterate. Because he knew that his nation trusted them and needed them. But when our resistance leaders come to the UN people, they have to prove that they have 'skills,' that they know how to read and how to write, that they speak the languages. There are no emotions involved, no respect for our past."

Many former FRETILIN fighters still hold to their arms and recent riots show how unstable the situation is. Called "extremist," the Marxist old guard of FRETILIN is heading for a clash with the present government that is going out of its way to please its mighty neighbors – Indonesia and Australia – and to reassure the United States that there is no left-wing philosophy engraved in the present leadership of the country.

In 2002 (then Presidential candidate) Gusmao explained to me that "a good relationship with Indonesia is a priority," that "people of East Timor should forget the recent past and look into the future," that they should "forgive." In the meantime, Indonesia never put one single high ranking official in prison for a substantial amount of time, in connection with the genocide in East Timor. There has been no official apology from Jakarta, not even one privately organized delegation from Indonesia that would take the pain of coming to Dili and offering condolences to the East Timorese people for what has been done to them.

With all due respect, President Gusmao is wrong. This sort of "reconciliation" based on silence never has never worked. It was tried in Argentina and in Chile after the dictatorship and it failed. It is an obligation of the East Timorese government to demand an official apology from Jakarta, to demand the opening of the Indonesian archives, and to demand that the Indonesian public be informed of the horrors inflicted on their country by its neighbors. Not for the purpose of revenge, but to help to heal the wounds of those who were and are suffering tremendous injustice.

The truth about the past is almost as important for Indonesia as it is for East Timor. Since 1965 when Indonesia endured massacres that took between 500 thousand and one million lives during the anti-Sukarno coup led by the pro-Suharto military clique (which lied to Indonesia and the world, claiming that it was fighting 'a Communist coup' that of course never took place), successive Indonesian leaders have managed to create myths and amnesia which are still plundering the nation's intellectual well being. Lies about 1965 were followed by lies about East Timor and later about Ambon, Iryan, Jaya, and Aceh.

It is insulting to tell East Timorese who survived rape, torture and loss of their loved ones that they should forget and forgive. Even if they would want to, they couldn't. Does anyone dare say to Poles, Russians, Yugoslavs, or the French right after the Second World War that they should just "forget and forgive"? And they lost relatively fewer people than the East Timorese. Could anyone be so cynical as to tell Jews who survived the Holocaust that they should "just forget it, forgive, and go on with their lives as if nothing really happened?"

And could they, could they ever forgive, after experiencing and witnessing some of the most barbaric acts ever committed by mankind? My Jewish friends who survived the Holocaust as children are still waking up in the middle of the night. And they scream, covered by cold sweat. And so do my East Timorese friends. And they still will twenty years, fifty years from now.

My liberal Indonesian friends tend to endlessly repeat that in fact the "East Timorese massacres would never have happened if the United States had not given the green light to the invasion." True. The United States, UK, Australia, all of us should live with the guilt for standing by, for not intervening while the occupation took place, for encouraging Indonesia to invade. We should speak about it, write about it as some of us (though not enough of us) do.

But this time it was not the United States that did the actual killing, raping, ethnic cleansing, and torturing. Should Soviets be blamed for Nazism because Stalin ordered the Communist Party of Germany to withdraw from the coalition with other leftists in an act that helped the Fascists win elections? To some extent, yes. But it was Germans who were designing the crematoriums and camps and it was their army that massacred tens of millions of men, women, and children.

The Indonesian people have to face up to their responsibilities. They have to acknowledge their own past, not only for the sake of their victims in East Timor, but also for the sake of their own future. No decent society can be built on lies. The past returns, it divides nations, it haunts, and eventually, if not faced honestly and with dignity, it kills.

Until the crimes are acknowledged, until there is a sincere apology and endless grief, until Indonesian children start learning at school that their nation massacred the innocent people of a small nation that never had a chance to resist but resisted nevertheless in one of the most heroic acts of defiance known to history, the old woman from Ermera with her back bent, will be climbing the hill, abandoned and forgotten, alone. Her government can suggest a thousand times that she should forget.

But the memory is all she has left; those whom she loved are all dead. Each day that goes by, each day that cameras should be showing the cynical grins of the untouchable Wiranto and other Indonesian generals, she will be descending deeper and deeper into her past, to her life brutally interrupted twenty years ago. I was not brave enough to stop her, too scared of the magnitude of pain that she was radiating.

August 2003

So Where Was the Resistance?

A few days before the Iraq war, we were promised massive anti-war demonstrations and public disobedience. Some analysts were predicting the collapse of European governments that decided to support the war, notably those in the United Kingdom and Spain.

London was supposed to be virtually shut down by angry crowds, "hundreds of bin-Ladens" were ready to strike at Western targets, according to the Egyptian government, and Indonesia was going to plunge into chaos. The war was likely to spread across the entire Middle East and the freedom loving people of the world were about to realize that the only way to preserve their way of life would be to unite and defend themselves against western aggression.

The Germans and the French, heads held high, set about rediscovering glorious words from their long-forgotten pasts.

All this was before the war. Although hardly anyone dared to believe that it could be prevented, some of us hoped that, if it happened, the entire universe would realize how cynical and perverted is a world ruled by a single superpower that increasingly regards itself to be beyond international law, and acts by a single ideology in the interests of a few rich nations.

To give credit where credit is due, millions of peace-loving men, women and children demonstrated against the war in Rome and London, in New York and Jakarta, in Mexico and Sydney.

Then the war began, and Prime Minister Blair's popularity soared. The protests in Australia diminished in size and frequency, and well over 70 percent of Americans (didn't we believe that the real resistance would start at home?) decided that the war deserved to be supported.

Two weeks after the beginning of our invasion of Iraq, most of the 'marching for peace' crowd were sitting in front of their televisions, eating peanuts, potato chips and popcorn, and gaping at CNN's interminable briefings from Doha Central Command and the Pentagon.

The great show rolled onwards, providing free entertainment to billions all over the globe. As predicted, Iraqi civilians were dying in large numbers, but the great majority of Americans, Europeans and others decided that wasn't worth the effort of putting on their shoes and marching against the invasion.

Just before the war ended, the French and German governments began toning down their criticism, sending reconciliatory messages to Washington DC along the lines of "We never really wanted Saddam to win" and "We're actually rather happy that the American and British forces are close to victory."

Now, several weeks after the war, devastated, divided and chaotic Iraq is almost forgotten, replaced on the television screens by SARS scares and natural disasters elsewhere in the world.

So, toward whom should the opposition direct its ire? At the United States, of course. At its allies, true. At Europe and Japan – the countries that don't like to fight but are always ready to enjoy the booty – definitely! But what about aiming our wrath at ourselves – at all of us who knew exactly what was going on but decided to watch instead of act?

Despite our frequent self-congratulatory speeches, we, the 'opposition', failed yet again – this time more then ever. While the Empire uses violence to suppress dissent anywhere in the world, we couldn't even organize one substantial general strike, or build one barricade in the centers of our capitals. Our opposition leaders are scared to 'call for violence' in case it might be labeled a 'terrorist act'. And, wow, aren't we afraid of that title now that we know what happens to those who are labeled that way! How long will it be before our governments start to designate high school students who protest against our invasions in far away places as 'terrorists'?

They can fight, bomb, maim and ruin, but we can't even break a few shop windows. Demonstrators are pushed back by tear gas, and their photos are taken. The truth is, it's not laziness that keeps us off the streets, it's fear!

We are afraid of being identified, of losing our jobs, of becoming unemployable, of being labeled by some unpleasant term, of becoming a target. These are uncertain times, after all.

But our fear is what the establishment counts upon. We are scared and divided. In many countries, the great majority of people apparently opposed the war. In Spain, for instance, the opposition counted for about 90 percent of the population. Where were these tens of millions of Spaniards then? Instead of boozing on Friday and Saturday, why didn't they take over Madrid and force the government of Aznar to resign? During the struggle against Pinochet, Chileans used to chant: "El pueblo unido jamas sera vencido" (The people united will never be defeated).

But there is no unity, anymore. It exists neither on a domestic level nor on an international one. And as long as it doesn't exist, the world order will continue to impose its designs on any nation of the world as it sees fit.

There are those who see progress in the creation of World Social Forums. One has to agree with them: it is a step forward. But these forums are too polite, often too theoretical. At the same time, the Western grip on world power is strengthening, is becoming firmer and firmer every year. The millions who are suffering under its remorseless totalitarianism can't wait forever. They are dying and starving, perishing from treatable illnesses, or working for a pittance in our sweatshops in Mexico and the Philippines.

If our legitimate opposition is not going to radicalize and unite itself, then the job will be done by extremists. And nobody wants that to happen!

At present, there is no plan and no philosophy on which our global opposition (if such a thing actually exists) could be based. Are we Marxists or just anti-racists? What kind of world do we want after the present structure collapses (if we ever succeed in making it collapse)? What global arrangement are we aiming for? What economic system are we advocating? Will the UN play the pre-eminent role in our new world or do we need new international institutions built from scratch? Without such plans, we can hardly count on mass support.

We are indisputably expert and vociferous critics, but how good are we at offering alternatives? Most of the issues that opposition thinkers are touching upon are mere details. Agreed, details are important, sometimes very important. But shouldn't we think about a master plan?

Opposition to the war against Iraq was painfully fragmented and poised to fail. It included such unlikely bedfellows as Chirac and Hugo Chavez, extreme Muslim groups and movements in Indonesia and the Communist Party of India, Greens in Europe and simple 'nice folks' back in the United States. Each 'faction' had its own agenda, each opposed the war for its own very different reasons.

The overwhelming majority of the world's population opposed the war but was unable to prevent it. It's time to ask, 'Why?' It's time to move from lofty postulations to concrete issues: to the tactics and strategy of future engagement and resistance.

There has to be coordination in the future. If the World Social Forum can coordinate an opposition, so be it. If it can't, something or someone else has to. It is obvious that

Iraq may be the beginning of a political transformation process, not the end. There will be other invasions, other terrible acts of our neo-colonialism. And they have to be stopped.

This time we failed patently and lamentably: our lack of cooperation, coordination and straightforward commitment meant that our vainglory was bound to fizzle out in worthless rhetoric. We deserved to fail. Now it's time to reflect and to plan. It's not good enough to echo what the Republicans in Spain used to say after losing to the fascists: "We lost, but we had better songs!"

June 2003

Indonesia - Not Even Yet At The Crossroad

There was no powerful scent of spring flowers in bloom in Jakarta. No girls wearing colorful light dresses, no miniskirts. No passionate embraces in front of the barricades, no guitars, almost no long hair.

Instead, there were burning buildings and shattered glass, tear gas and a constant howling of ambulances and police cars, fists pointing to the sky in anger and defiance. There appeared to be a revolution in the making, an unmistakable desire for change, a hunger for a better country – a more honest, more livable country.

One day on the streets of Jakarta, police shot and killed students at the Trisakti University, one of the country's elite schools, and Jakarta erupted in spontaneous revolt against President Suharto's US-backed dictatorship. Students stood at the vanguard, soon to be followed by the frustrated masses, surprisingly including members of an already shrinking middle class.

The whole world watched images of the fourth most populous nation on earth revolting against a brutal and corrupt regime: according to some, Indonesia was fighting for freedom, while others believed it was descending into anarchy, becoming ungovernable, and heading rapidly toward disintegration.

Protesting Jakarta have-nots trashed Chinese businesses, raped women and looted stores, carrying off everything from refrigerators to shoes. There was chaos on the streets, and it soon became evident that, even if there had been some leadership trying to coordinate the uprising, it had lost control over the crowd.

At that point I met the leaders of the student revolt in a computer room at the Trisakti University, hastily converted into the headquarters of an uprising against the regime. One of them was called Suresh. He seemed a gentle human being, well brought up, well mannered. His eyes were red from lack of sleep, his shaking fingers holding a clove cigarette, his shirt unwashed for days.

After our first meeting, I abandoned my comfortable hotel room and moved to the HQ, sleeping as they did under tables and wires on the floor, participating in their countless meetings, trying to understand exactly what had prompted them to put their lives on the line, to fight for change in their enormous, complex and wounded country.

At one point I abandoned my dislike of clichés and asked the student leader: "So this is your Sorbonne, your Paris, your Mexico City of 1968, isn't it?"

What followed was a long silence.

"You're wrong," he finally answered. "In the West, they fought for 'free love' and revolted against their parents, their families, their professors, and their culture. We love our country, we love and respect our families and our teachers. We are dying to return to our homes and to our classrooms, we are tired and confused. All we want is our country to return to the rule of law: we want an end to corruption and we want justice."

It was an honest answer, confirming my suspicions formed by following earlier riots on the streets. This was no revolution, just a rebellion that was to doom Indonesia for at least another decade and ensure that nothing would essentially change in the foreseeable future.

Soon after, Suharto's regime collapsed. Six years later, Indonesia is still a stubbornly conservative country ruled by a minuscule clique made up of individuals motivated by private interests and backed by the might of the military.

Recently, Indonesia introduced two seemingly unrelated laws. One banned cohabitation (men and women are not allowed to live together unless they are related or married), and the other reconfirmed an existing law implemented in 1966 banning Communist Parties, particularly the PKI.

The PKI was first outlawed after Suharto's 1965 coup against Sukarno, an act supported by the US. The human cost has been estimated to be between 500 thousand and 1.2 million lives. Generally supportive of Sukarno, the Communist Party was singled out and falsely accused of staging the coup (in fact, it had been instigated by Suharto and his military faction). Its members were promptly liquidated en masse. Among the victims were also members of the Chinese minority (who were absurdly accused of supporting Communist China), opponents of the new regime, and progressive thinkers, as well as professors and intellectuals in general.

Demanding full obedience, the dictatorship saw intellectual and creative activities as the most dangerous challenge to its rule.

While tolerating and even promoting local culture (mainly folk music and dance) as well as pop of any origin as long as it carried no 'subversive messages', Indonesia embarked on a long and painful process of intellectual degradation.

Chinese culture, language and even characters were (and still are) banned. The educational system discouraged any creativity and espoused the most vulgar state propaganda. Nationalism was promoted avidly. Even in Jakarta, there was almost no access to the works of foreign (except Hollywood) filmmakers. Writers such as Promoedya Ananta Toer were thrown into concentration camps.

The two pillars of the system became 'religion' and 'the family'. To lack religion became illegal behavior: everybody had to (and still must) commit to one of the five officially sanctioned religions on his or her identity card (Muslim, Catholic, Protestant, Buddhist or Hindu).

In addition to its military and police resources, as well as its secret services, the regime needed some well organized 'moderate' forces to help it keep the population in a manageable and governable state. It was a strictly pragmatic move – Suharto himself was no great believer.

As in almost all poor countries ruled by extreme right wing governments with almost no social spending, the concept of a 'strong family' unit became a decisively important socio-economic element. Parents were expected to make great sacrifices to educate and support their children, who were later expected to support their aging parents (identical to the situation in Latin America or Africa).

Two or more generations crammed into a single house was supposed to demonstrate 'love between the family members' instead of a lack of independent and affordable housing. Families accepted the deceit: they had no choice. Internal family support became an almost exclusive way for the survival of its members.

The linguistics of the process were turned upside down. Necessity was turned into virtue, the way to survive into 'family love'.

While the government liquidated the leftovers of the intellectuals and free thinkers, children were encouraged to dance traditional dances and sing folk songs, love their country and not contradict their elders and teachers.

A God-fearing nation was the next logical step. Sukarno's secularism had not been destroyed. Even now, Indonesia remains a secular country in many ways. Nevertheless, in a society where almost any alternative thought or criticism of the system led to some sort of discrimination, sanctions or something much worse, religion became almost the only escape from a dreary reality.

Religion was whole-heartedly encouraged. The government tactic was not to force people into mosques, temples or churches. Instead, it banned anyone who refused to accept one of the 'official' faiths. Those who refused to lie about their life philosophy by endorsing a faith were often labeled as 'communists' (akin to a devil in Suharto's lexicon). Children were initiated into religion at an early age: no parent would dare to do otherwise, fearing tremendous stigmatization of their offspring.

Moving dramatically from a relaxed approach to religion during Sukarno's rule, post-1965 Indonesia embraced religion as a sort of public display of loyalty and conformity, instead of a personal and extremely private expression of faith. Suharto's departure made no difference: indeed, new strictures such as a dress code for women (something very relaxed in the past) and strict observance of all religious rules became issues. The 'system' did not interfere in the process; as far as it was concerned, women could wear anything they wanted.

But society itself, oppressed and not even able to remember what it meant to think independently, took up the role of arbitrator, regulator and that of a moral judge. Today's dress code is not forced upon women by the government, nor even by Islam or other religions: it is 'expected' by society itself, by family members, co-workers, neighbors and friends. In a generally unpleasant social, political and economic climate, one is expected to find 'happiness' in religion, instead of in day-to-day life.

One counter-argument would be: "but if they like it that way, why challenge their choice?" The answer is, "because they never had a choice." Almost no child comes in touch with any alternative to religion (for instance, the theory of evolution is mentioned only to be ridiculed) and society destroys anyone who openly refuses to follow a faith – 'breaking the heart of the family' a euphemism for probable excommunication from their kith and kin.

The 1965 massacres were never openly and publicly discussed. Most Indonesians are unaware of the massacres in East Timor, believing that "we were killing them and they were killing us." Families have no influence upon changing their structure due to economic and housing conditions. The present economic system is sacrosanct because the alternative would be 'communism', and thus illegal.

The system has become almost perfect in many ways. There is no longer a need for a huge police force or an army of informants. Any truly fundamental opposition is labeled as leftist or communist and either dismissed or simply banned. 'Family values' and religion assure conformity of the members of Indonesian society at the basic level, negating any effort of men and women to live unique and independent lives – behavior regarded as 'dangerous' and therefore a threat to the status quo.

Education offers repetitiveness and uniformity. A more open culture expressed in critical written words or films (Indonesia has almost no film production considering its size) was destroyed many years ago. Any deviation by an individual from the 'norm' is condemned by the members of the society itself!

Many brilliant minds gave up (or never had a chance to bloom), mostly entering 'business' as the only way to succeed (thereby further strengthening the system), instead of embarking on a discouraged path of creativity. Responses to such limitations are designed simply to make families 'happy' or are practical, based on a need to provide for themselves and their families or because their uniqueness or creativity cannot be recognized (for instance, how can one excel in arts if any discussion or argument is discouraged in advance even at the university?). Of course, not to be pro-business would automatically cause people to be labeled with the 'c' word in any case!!!

Fatherland, religion, family, business: the four columns that support one of the most stagnant, poor and socially uneven nations of Pacific Asia – once a nation of limitless potential due to its natural resources and, yes, exactly due to the culture and creativity of its people!

Fiercely critical of the US and its foreign policy (over 50 percent of Indonesians believe that Osama bin Laden has "something to offer" the world), the Indonesian state increasingly resembles a sort of 'dirt poor' version of the nightmare of any progressively thinking citizen in the United States.

If Indonesians could vote in the next American election, they would almost definitely vote for the current US President, George Bush. Like him, Indonesians are generally pro-death penalty, anti-abortion, anti-cloning, anti-legalization of soft drugs and anti-Communist. They are God fearing, 'family oriented' and patriotic. On some issues, they would go even further than Bush, by being fundamentally anti-gay and lesbian and against mixed marriages.

Indonesia makes sure that any foreigner who marries an Indonesian citizen has a miserable life. Even to contemplate a marriage acceptable to the family and the state, those who have no religion have to commit to convert to a recognized faith.

By supporting the 1965 coup and the regime that followed, we helped to create something that went even beyond our wildest expectations. Not only has the legacy of the progressive, secular and non-allied Sukarno been destroyed, but what followed was a strictly pro-business, socially indifferent, extremely conservative and outrageously moralistic society generating barely 1,000 dollars per capita in GDP. That's quite an 'achievement', considering that pre-1965 Indonesia was one of the brightest hopes of the developing world!

Patriotism sometimes gives way to realism. Off the shore of the island of Lombok, I was once told by the local fishermen: "If we, the poor people of Indonesia, could…we would all leave for Australia, Singapore, the US, or Europe. Only the rich like it here, because they can have us almost for free. But even they would have to leave, because with us gone, they would have to learn how to clean and cook and do everything by themselves."

After a few years, I would like to meet Suresh again and ask him a few questions: "Wouldn't it be more comfortable to have the women of Jakarta wearing light summer dresses in the tropical heat? Wouldn't it be more acceptable to have a bit of what you called 'free sex'? Wouldn't it be better to challenge parents and teachers in order to make some fundamental changes in society instead of having the present anti-cohabitation and anti-communist laws, instead of the never-ending corruption and exploitation, instead of the fear and self-censorship often imposed by the inertia of society itself? Wouldn't a real revolution be better than the present state of affairs?"

December 2003

Alberto Fujimori And Japanese Racism

In 1993, one year after the 'self-coup' performed by Alberto Fujimori, his supporters and the military, the office of 'Coordinadora nacional de los derechos humanos' ('National Coordination Office for Human Rights') in Lima was packed with desperate old women, arriving from every corner of the country. They were holding old photographs of their sons and daughters who had disappeared in recent months and years.

The Director of the office, corpulent, determined and overworked Francisco Soberon and his staff were desperately trying to record information, to file petitions, and inform the foreign press about the situation. Thousands of people were missing, some unaccounted for, some rotting alive at cold, high altitude, high security prisons around Puno and elsewhere having been convicted in emergency trials conducted by judges with their heads and faces covered by masks. The army, police and intelligence services were continuing to rape and torture, to perform extra-judiciary executions, and to 'disappear' people who were accused of supporting 'terrorism' (read: Maoist 'Shining Path' and Marxists 'MRTA').

And Alberto Fujimori, President of Peru – agrarian engineer of Japanese descent – and his intelligence chief Vladimiro Montesinos, were in charge!

By then, the civil or 'dirty' war was already officially over, with the leaders of both Shining Path and MRTA behind bars. But the witch-hunt continued: people were still dying and disappearing, and the army ruled the mountains, coast and jungle through fear and terror.

Japan continued to provide unconditional generous assistance to this Andean country or, more accurately, to its dictatorship. In the past, it had rarely shown generosity toward South America, despite exporting hundreds of thousands of economic refugees into its countries in the past (today, there is well over a million people of Japanese descent living in Brazil and Peru). When Fujimori became President, everything changed. He was of Japanese stock, after all! There was Japanese blood flowing through his veins!

When the MRTA rebels took over the Japanese Ambassador's residency in Lima during a lavish party to celebrate the Emperor's birthday, almost the entire Japanese nation were in no doubt that what was happening was an act of terrorism against their country. At that time, I was working in Lima for Asahi Shimbun – a large Tokyo daily. The news and information flowing from Peru through the Japanese media was being carefully 'moderated' to take the 'sensitivity' of the topic into consideration.

Still, even so we managed to interview and put on the record the words of Otilia Campos de Polay, the mother of Victor Polay, the then imprisoned leader of MRTA, herself an important figure in Peruvian politics and a co-founder of one of the largest political parties – APRA. She sent this message to the Japanese public: "I know your country well. I visited your ancient cities, saw your holy mountains. Once you were poor and we were rich. Your people came here to live and they were accepted. Now you are rich and we are dirt poor. And you are supporting the dictatorship in our country. Why? Please try to understand our people…"

Fujimori had no interest in solving the problem. He suppressed the information from our interview with MRTA where they declared that all they wanted was to improve conditions of the poor and to be legalized as a political opposition party. He directed the kidnapping of several men from the rescue brigade of the highest mine in the world – Cerro de Pasqua – and ordered them to dig tunnels under the Japanese compound. In April 1997, he ordered an attack which led to killing of all the MRTA members, including a pregnant girl who was shot at point blank range while begging for mercy.

Despite the fact that this act was contrary to all the Japanese government plans, it was never publicly condemned by Japan.

Fujimori tried his best to be a good friend of the United States by his 'war against terrorism' and his 'war on drugs'. And it paid off! His excesses were forgiven by the 'North', his human rights record mostly overlooked.

Many Peruvians, tired of a civil war that had cost at least 35 thousand lives and dispirited by the disastrous economic performance of Fujimori's corrupt predecessor – APRA President Alan Garcia – were willing to accept his 'iron-fist' rule for many years. He defeated the two left-wing movements and curbed hyper-inflation.

However, the price of the 'victory' was tremendous: the kidnapping and murders (apparently, Fujimori was fully aware of the existence of the 'death squad' known as 'The Grupo Colina'), the torture (he didn't hesitate to order the arrest of his wife who publicly criticized his policies – she was then tortured in detention), the growing social disparities, the uncontrollable corruption, and his dark political designs that almost led to a full blown war with Peru's neighbor Ecuador. He controlled the mass media and intimidated and spied on his political opponents. He rewrote the constitution and stuffed Congress with his own supporters.

Yet still Japan stood aside, offering moral and financial support.

When the 'irregularities' became blatantly obvious before the May 2000 elections, even the United States and the Organization of American States expressed their concern. When the then spy-chief Vladimiro Montesinos was caught bribing a Congressman on tape, all hell broke loose. The opposition gained ground and dismissed Fujimori on the grounds of his 'moral incapacity'.

Fujimori fled to Japan and, to save face, tendered his resignation. Congress refused the offer, and insisted on dismissing him instead.

For more than a decade, Fujimori's nationality had been a mystery. According to the Peruvian constitution, only a person born in Peru could become the country's president. Fujimori's birth certificate had mysteriously 'disappeared'. As part of my work for Asahi Shimbun, we launched an investigation in Japan, trying to find out whether the certificate existed there, while almost all Peruvian newspapers embarked on searches in their home country. The result was nil. It was widely believed that the secret of Fujimori's birth was known only to Montesinos, who was therefore in position to blackmail the president and exercise enormous power. According to one theory, Fujimori was born on the boat between Japan and Peru.

The former dictator received a warm welcome in Japan and was granted Japanese citizenship almost immediately. When the Peruvian ambassador to Tokyo – Luis Macchiavello – presented a 700-page extradition request, it was met by a humiliating silence. A later request by Interpol met a similar fate. Japan declared that it had no extradition treaty with Peru, and the Japanese Foreign Ministry said that "We will follow only our domestic laws in deciding how to respond."

Many people in Peru and other countries in South America found Tokyo's response insulting. The extradition request had been based on well-documented cases that accused Fujimori, among other things, of being involved in the killing of suspected leftist rebels in Lima in 1991, in the kidnapping and killing of nine students and a professor from La Cantuta University in 1992, and in giving Montesinos $15 million in severance pay.

In March, Interpol placed Fujimori on its most-wanted list and Peruvian prosecutors threatened to take the case to the

International Court of Justice if Japan continued in its obduracy. The only response from Tokyo was that "Japan has no plan to take any sort of action against Mr. Fujimori at this moment."

By July, Fujimori was laughing and ridiculing the entire extradition process. He declared in Tokyo that he would one day return to Peru, not to stand trial but to head a new Peruvian party – 'Si Cumple' ('Yes, he fulfills promises').

In Japan, Fujimori is barely recognized as a dictator. The mass media present him as reformist, a fighter against terrorism and, of course, Japanese by blood. At present, there are no serious inquiries or protests by the Japanese public against the treatment of a South American country that once accepted thousands of desperate Japanese immigrants and later became torn by brutal civil war.

Tokyo's approach is, without doubt, patronizing, humiliating and racist. It shows indifference to the crimes committed by a man who is now holding Japanese citizenship; crimes in which Japan is also implicated by its support for his dictatorship from beginning to end. It is outrageous that, in many 'developed countries', when blood ties are involved, justice and morality become irrelevant.

February 2004

Thailand: What's Going On?

On Wednesday April 28th, more than a hundred militants clashed with Thai security forces in the three impoverished southern provinces of Yala, Pattani and Songkhla near the Malaysian border. They apparently launched coordinated attacks on ten police stations. Almost all the militants were young, teenagers by some accounts, and many wore Islamic slogans. The attackers were poorly armed – most of them brandished machetes, and only a handful had guns.

Despite their minimal weaponry, almost all of the militants were killed/slaughtered by the security forces. To escape the carnage, 32 of the 'rebels' took shelter in one of the oldest and most important mosques in the country, located on the outskirts of the provincial capital of Pattani. After a six-hour stand-off, troops stormed the mosque, indiscriminately killing everyone inside. Overall, at least 107 rebels and 5 soldiers died during the battle.

Thailand has a long history stretching back to the 1970s and 1980s of Islamic separatist insurgency in its southern and predominantly Muslim provinces. In recent months, there had been several bloody attacks on security installations prior to the incidents on April 28th.

The Thai Prime Minister, Thaksin Shinawatra, immediately labeled the insurgents as 'criminals', playing down any religious or ideological motives, and vowing to smash 'the ring of troublemakers'. Army chief General Chaiyasidh Shinawatra admitted that the intelligence services had been tipped off in advance of the attacks and there is no doubt that the security forces were expecting trouble and were prepared for a violent response.

Thailand looks less and less like the image it tries to project to the rest of the world – a tranquil paradise in the middle of a troubled region. Its present government is increasingly embracing brutal tactics akin to those used by military dictatorships in other parts of the world. The Thai military, although utterly ineffective in fighting foreign enemies (in the past they were even defeated in a short border war with Laos), is both powerful and influential internally, as are the police and other branches of the security forces.

Prime Minister Thaksin clearly belongs to the breed of populist politicians in the region who believe that any member of an insurgency, as well as any drug dealer, deserves the same treatment: extrajudicial execution.

To make matters worse, Thaksin Shinawatra doesn't just talk, he acts! His war on drugs cost at least 2,000 lives in the first months of 2003 (detailed statistics became blurry) causing uproar among human rights organizations at home and abroad. The 'concept' was straightforward: drug dealers were to be taken dead or alive, and the security forces were promised extra bonuses for each body supplied.

Inevitably, the security forces went out of their way to deliver the goods. Their work ethic increased dramatically – undeniably confirmed by the piles of bodies of alleged drug dealers, many of whom were destitute illegal immigrants from Cambodia and elsewhere. Strangely, almost no 'drug dealers' were captured alive. Many analysts considered that the security forces were simply murdering defenseless poor people in order to earn extra cash.

The Thai government (this time, to be fair, with the active involvement of its Cambodian counterpart) led its country into an extremely tense situation with its neighbor following anti-Thai riots in the capital Phnom Penh. It also ordered a 'cleaning-up operation' to rid the streets of Bangkok of beggars and homeless people on the eve of President Bush's arrival. Add a brutal repatriation policy that is sending thousands of Burmese refugees, many HIV positive, to certain death across the border, and the picture of Thailand becomes much less attractive.

How can Thailand get away with all this and still preserve its reputation as a calm and friendly country? Probably the main reason is the Western media's historical reluctance to criticize a country that has been for decades a dependable servant of the West, and particularly of the United States.

Thailand 'took care' of its 'Communist problem' by effective methods that included burning insurgents alive in oil drums and dropping them alive from helicopters (yes, not unlike in Chile under Pinochet!). It offered its land and women to the

American army during the Vietnam War (that's how Pattaya, formerly a US military base, was transformed into the jewel in the crown of today's sex tourism industry).

It did plenty of dirty work for the US in the Vietnam, Laos and Cambodia operations that couldn't gain approval even from the US Congress.

Despite outward appearances, linguistically and culturally unique and hermetic Thailand remains a relatively closed society, hard to understand by those who haven't mastered the language and spent long years on its territory.

This time, the government and security forces' harsh approach may yet backfire. The situation in the south is tense and explosive, and the provinces where the insurgency occurred are poor and desperate. It is obvious that not all attempts to solve the stand-off peacefully were exhausted. In fact, it is doubtful that there were any attempts at all. To the majority of Muslims, the desecration of the mosque and the merciless slaughter on its premises are a deep and barbaric affront to Islam.

The death toll, more than a hundred insurgents killed compared with five from the security forces, speaks clearly about the security forces' overwhelming firepower. There appears to be no justification for the massacre in the mosque apart from a desire by the Thai forces to conceal something important or, more likely, to send a brutal 'message' to Muslims.

Relations between Thailand and Malaysia remain tense. Worldwide, and in Southeast Asia in particular, these are uncertain and difficult times – it is quite possible that the large Muslim community in the countries of this region will act unpredictably. The worst one can do is to stir passions and escalate conflicts.

It is painfully obvious that the sensible course for the Thai government is to listen to the valid grievances of its people and discontinue its current bullish strategy. It should negotiate and seek solutions. If it fails to do so, Thailand's southern region may become yet another battlefield, not unlike those in the southern Philippines, Aceh and Ambon.

May 2004

East Timor – Australia's Shame

What can you do if your country is tiny and poor and your wealthy neighbor shamelessly exploits a commonly shared area rich in natural resources depriving you of funds so much needed to feed your people?

East Timor, Asia's poorest nation that recently celebrated its second anniversary of independence is still desperate and unable to feed itself. Almost half of its population is unemployed and at least half is illiterate.

Right from the beginning, East Timor also feels deeply humiliated by its mighty neighbor – Australia. Both countries are locked in a long, bitter dispute over enormous oil and gas reserves beneath the Timor Sea.

Potential profits from this reserve are so high that, if fairly divided, they could easily guarantee East Timor's full economic self-sufficiency and tackle most of its urgent social problems.

However, Australia opted for a bullish and intimidating approach, disregarding international law, often openly and directly laughing in the face of a relatively helpless East Timorese government. Until now, it accepts only one border agreement signed by Suharto's government and Australia during the time when East Timor was still firmly under brutal Indonesian occupation.

The Economist, a British weekly news magazine, summarized the situation by saying:

> Some of the disputed resources lie in a zone known as the Timor Gap that Australia and Indonesia excluded when they delineated their seabed boundary in 1972. Seventeen years later the two countries signed a deal to divide government revenues from this zone evenly between them. Mr. Gusmao now describes that deal as 'illegal and illegitimate' because of Indonesia's occupation of East Timor at the time.
>
> At independence, Australia signed an interim treaty with East Timor, giving the nation 90 percent of revenues from within the 'joint development area', as the gap is now called, and Australia 10 percent. This agreement covers the Bayu-Undan gas field, due to start production this year. But it excludes most of Greater Sunrise, a more lucrative gas field that lies mostly outside the area, and all of the Laminaria-Corallina oil field, from which Australia has been taking all revenues since it started pumping in 1999.

The President of East Timor, Xanana Gusmao, offered several solutions, one of them being potential arbitration by a third party. However, Australia refused to negotiate. Arbitration by the International Court of Justice is now also impossible, because Australia withdrew from its jurisdiction on maritime boundary questions right before East Timor gained independence.

East Timorese Prime Minister Mari Alkatiri claims that "East Timor would get access to as much as US $12 billion worth of oil and gas" if the resources would be divided fairly. For the present time, his government is suggesting that Australia and East Timor form an escrow account into which money from oil and gas exploration will be deposited until the issue is resolved. But, according to *The Star*, an Australian newspaper, "Australia refuses to accept a maritime boundary in the middle of the 600 miles of sea separating the two countries" – exactly what East Timor is demanding.

In the meantime, the Australian government is using insulting language toward its East Timorese counterpart. Alexander Downer recently declared on the Australian Broadcasting Corporation (ABC) News: "East Timor's poverty is no reason for Australia to give ground in a maritime border dispute involving energy reserves. With the greatest of respect, grow up. We are enormously rich compared to Papua New Guinea. We would be six or seven times richer than New Zealand. That doesn't mean that the solution to that problem is to cede a lot of our territory to those countries. You address that issue of economic disparity through your aid program."

And aid programs there are, including coming from Australia. However, they amount to approximately 10 percent of the profits made by Australia from exploring gas and oil in the disputed area. And exploration is only at an infantile stage.

After the fruitless April meeting between the two governments (East Timor is insisting on monthly meetings, but Australia agreed to only two meetings per year, therefore the next one will not take place before September), Alexander Downer threatened: "East Timor made a very big mistake trying to shame Australia, accusing us of being bullying and rich and so on, considering all we've done for East Timor."

Australia likes to brag about its "help" to East Timor, often forgetting about the not too distant past.

In February 1942 the Japanese Imperial Army landed an army of 20 thousand men in Dili (the capital of East Timor) and occupied the then Portuguese colony. The Japanese were ready to launch an attack on Australia from there. East Timorese, alongside a small Australian force, fought fiercely against Japanese invaders, inflicting tremendous losses. This resistance is often described as an act that saved Australia from a terrible war on its own territory.

After Australians were evacuated, the Japanese performed terrible revenge. The population of East Timor declined from 472 thousand in 1930 to 403 thousand in 1946 (the two closest available censuses).

After gaining short-lived independence from Portugal, East Timor was occupied by Indonesian troops on December 7,

1975. During the occupation, the country lost more than one third of its population in one of the most brutal genocides known to the 20th century. The US and Australia gave an unmistakable green light to Suharto and his military clique. Until now, East Timor has received no substantial compensation from Indonesia or from those countries that encouraged the invasion.

It is true that Australia led a multinational force that helped East Timor after the independence referendum and consequent massacres by pro-Jakarta militias. However, Australia's withdrawal from the International Court of Justice's jurisdiction on maritime boundary questions just before the full independence of East Timor may lead to many unfavorable speculations about the motives for such help. It is easier to bully a small and defenseless nation over the issue of enormous natural resources, than to confront the fourth most populous nation on earth – Indonesia.

760 thousand people of East Timor, descendants of those who survived colonial neglect and terrible invasions and occupations, form the poorest nation in Asia. The country is too far from the main focus of cameras belonging to the large broadcasting corporations. Few journalists bother to venture to the far corner of the earth where it is located. It has no navy and no air-force to defend its interests.

But it has oil and gas that can pay for new schools and hospitals, roads, and housing. East Timor doesn't need aid – it needs a fair deal arbitrated by international institutions. The trouble is that it is being told, directly and squarely, by its mighty neighbor to 'forget about it', to take what it's being offered (a pittance) and shut up. And it seems that no international body is able or willing to challenge a huge economic power like Australia, no matter how wrong it may be, how arrogantly and unjustly it behaves.

"We are not shaming Australia. We are only telling the truth," said Mr. Gusmao, recently. The question is whether anyone is willing to listen and above all, to take action in defense of the penniless but proud nation that suffered tremendously due to our geo-political interests.

June 2004

Will Indonesia Be Saved By "Euro - 2004"?

It appears on Indonesian television almost every night: huge red banner advertisements for Gudang Garam, a popular local brand of clove cigarettes, backed by the roar of football fans. 'Euro-2004' live from Portugal has begun!

Regardless of the late hour, millions of Indonesian men, women and children are glued to their screens. Most televised matches kick off around 1:45 a.m. in Jakarta or 2:45 a.m. in Bali, complete with an English commentary. Even though the Indonesian national team has never come close to qualifying for any important football event apart from the Asian Games, the entire nation is obsessed, hooked on adrenalin and drunk with vicarious glory from a spectacle beamed halfway across the world.

Like soap operas, often imported from dubious production companies in Latin America, football evokes tremendous passion in this fourth most populous nation on earth. Indonesians know everything there is to know about the leading players in the European teams, be they Dutch, German, Italian, British or whatever, and discuss football strategies at home and at the office with the confidence of professional match analysts.

Growing up in the western part of Czechoslovakia, now the Czech Republic, I used to play football as a child. Not very well, but I played – as did everyone else. After moving to New York, I lost touch with the world's most popular sporting activity – I gave up following particular teams, and even forgot most of the rules. But Indonesia, where I now work, made sure of reminding me.

Text messages such as "So which team are you supporting?" began appearing on my mobile phone. At first, I thought it was a joke, sarcastic questions for a sporting ignoramus obsessed with politics. With Indonesia less than a fortnight from crucial Presidential elections threatening a victory by one of two army generals, a result that could easily plunge this country back into the dark days, it seemed a likely explanation. Or maybe the enigmatic missives were ironic – comments on the insane behavior of the United States and British troops in Iraq? But no! It soon became apparent that my friends were deadly serious and the messages meant one thing only: football!

At first, I affected to refuse to follow the games, attempting to discuss local and world affairs instead, but that didn't make me feel very popular. I was out of line and out of place: boring, thoroughly 'out of it'. I thus decided to adopt a 'my team' strategy and settled upon the seemingly most benign and insignificant, the Czech Republic, certain losers in the company of such giants as Holland, France, Germany and Great Britain.

The people of Indonesia almost exclusively lined up behind their old colonizers – the Dutch. No matter that Holland had plundered the resources of this archipelago for centuries. No matter that it left almost nothing in exchange except poverty and underdevelopment. Regardless of events in the past, the Dutch team members were the chosen heroes of this unfortunate nation.

In Group D, the Czechs defeated Latvia and followed up with a roaring victory over Holland! Did I feel proud? You bet I did! I had no idea why: I haven't lived there for twenty years. I hold US citizenship, and visit my country of birth once a year, at most. Not being fully Czech by blood, my childhood there was close to miserable. But suddenly, the Czech Republic was 'my team', and next 'The team' of the tournament, winning one game after another!

Then came that glorious game against Germany: hordes of Czech fans, all in red, waving their banners with obscure and hard to pronounce village names, drumming their support, and singing until they were hoarse. Germany, knowing that anything short of victory meant certain elimination from the tournament, was desperate to win but made one error after another. They scored first, but the Czechs replied. Then, in the second half, the Czechs slammed in another goal.

In Bali, at almost 4 a.m., I too was glued to the television. My pulse was racing and my consumption of coffee and cigarettes had rocketed. Before the game, I had been corresponding with the New York Independent Film Festival and the San Sebastian Film Festival in Spain about my documentary film exposing the crimes during Suharto's term as Indonesia's President. I was waiting for the answer from my literary agent in New York about my latest book. But all that suddenly seemed trivial: the Czechs were beating the Germans!

The fans in the stadium were separated, each group giving loud and full-hearted support to their team. It looked like a war zone, an event of utmost significance equivalent to the time when a Czechoslovak team played the Soviet Union in an ice hockey tournament after the 1968 occupation. Forget about the fact that the Czechs showed no serious resistance to the Soviets as they never fought Nazi invaders, except in the last few days of the war when the outcome was already determined. Yes, forget about the history: this was much more glorious – this epic football match – eleven heroes on each side chasing one ball, trying to propel it between two vertical, and one horizontal, poles!

Then it was all over – the Germans had lost 2 to 1. They were 'out', humiliated, beaten, defeated. The cameras showed several German fans – some crying, some with enormous pain engraved on their faces. Their dreams were shattered. I suddenly felt sorry for them: I really did! Of course, 'my team' had won so I could afford a dose of goodwill.

A few days earlier, hardly any German voters had bothered to vote in important EU elections, an indication that the nation was clearly dissatisfied and disillusioned with the political system. But then, there was no sadness on German streets and on the faces of ordinary people. Now there was!

While the Czechs and Germans were locked in their epic battle, Holland beat Latvia and narrowly qualified for the quarterfinals. Many Indonesians regained the hopes dashed by 'my team's' win over 'their team' earlier in the competition: in the morning light, life on the Indonesian archipelago seemed much better, fuller and meaningful.

There were some small blemishes, of course. Malaysian cities were choking from the smoke coming from illegal logging in Indonesian Sumatra. The numbers of child prostitutes and beggars were increasing in all major urban centers, economic growth was stubbornly refusing to follow inflation, censorship was becoming even more repressive, corruption was out of control and there was no opposition candidate willing to represent the miserable and silent majority of the people in the upcoming elections.

But all that pales into insignificance while eleven Dutch boys, most of whom are known by name by Indonesians, are still competing in Euro-2004. As long as they remain on the path to glory, the familiar cigarette advertisements will flash across the screens, and the deafening roar of football fans will overwhelm the doubts and fears of people living on these distant shores.

It will all culminate on July 5th (Indonesian time) when the Indonesian presidential elections and Euro-2004 reach their respective climaxes on the same day. Will the Czechs make it? Will the Dutch hold the trophy aloft? Will Indonesia go back to the days of fear and darkness and hopelessness? Together with millions of Indonesians, I will be watching these momentous events.

July 2004

Is It Wrong To Defend Najaf?

Najaf – a Shia holy city in Iraq is turning once again into a battlefield. Thousands of supporters of cleric Moqtada al-Sadr now control the shrine, one of the holiest places of Shia Muslims, as well as the streets around it. US forces are attacking from the ground and from the air, inflicting heavy casualties. Hundreds of defenders of Najaf have already been killed and Al-Sadr himself was wounded. The war in Iraq continues.

The western press labels Mr. Sadr as "radical" and "anti-American." He is quoted as saying that the United States is intent on "occupying the whole world," adding that "The presence of occupation in Iraq has made our country an unbearable hell."

He also pledged to fight the occupation forces until his last drop of blood; his own blood, not just the blood of his supporters.

All this is understandable. History knows almost no case of occupation that did not encounter strong resistance. French and Polish resistance fought against Germans during WWII. Hungarians fought the Soviet Red Army in the 1950's and the Vietnamese people were defending themselves against the overwhelming American invasion force. Palestinians continue fighting the Israeli army. On the other hand, every occupation force, past and present, tries to destroy resistance, demonizing it in the process, labeling its members as "radicals," "extremists," even "terrorists."

So why are we suddenly so surprised now when this familiar situation occurs in Iraq – a previously independent country that we ruthlessly overrun, after some false presumptions and outright lies? Why are we shocked by the vigor of the resistance to our armed forces and the puppet government?

To clean the record, it's not that Al-Sadr is particularly "anti-American," as the official press lately enjoys calling him (again, no surprise, since we call "Anti-American" and "radical" everyone who stands against our global designs). To mark Ramadan on November 6, 2003, he sent a letter to the occupation forces that states: "I hope you will send my greetings and my thanks to the American people who love peace. I thank them because they supported us by demonstrations. I love them because I want to guide them to God and I wish to unify them with our people."

Almost one year later, there seems to be no chance for a peaceful settlement. The occupation continues, despite any half-hearted "transfer of power"; atrocities by the occupation forces at prisons and detention centers have been unveiled; security is collapsing and the majority of Iraqis are now living in unimaginable misery and hopelessness.

In this political, military and social climate, Al-Sadr called on his supporters to fight against the occupation and to defend their city, and he promised to lead personally the revolt and spill his own blood.

As an agnostic, I may have some great difficulties understanding Al-Sadr's religious motives for this revolt. However, no matter from what angle I look at the situation, I understand why he chose to defend his own city against the foreign invasion.

Before the fighting began, al-Sadr made an unusually civil statement, saying that those who are ready to stay and fight on his side are welcome and those who want to leave are welcome to do so as well.

In the modern world, his statements and approach are almost unprecedented. In the time of conflicts, our leaders are always ready to sacrifice thousands and millions of people for their own goals, never risking their own precious lives. This is true of our enemies (Mr. Hussein and Mr. Bin-Laden) as well as of our own allies (the same Mr. Hussein when he was still on our payroll, as well as the Generals Suharto and Pinochet, to name just a few).

It is also true of our own leaders. Who could ever forget that long and embarrassing silence when the US President and Commander-in-Chief learned that our country had been attacked on September 11th? He finished his infantile reading and went into hiding, becoming virtually incommunicado. Did we ever hear from him that he was flying immediately to New York City or Washington, ready to spill his blood to personally supervise the defense of the cities so dear to this nation?

Of those who went to fight to far away places in Afghanistan, Vietnam, Iraq, Panama or Grenada; how many were top ranking political, economic or even religious leaders? How many of those were their children?

To achieve a permanent peace, we should probably demand that in case we decide to go to war, our elites and their children would lead the soldiers into battle. If they so strongly believe in the causes that we are "defending" all over the world, they should be ready to abandon their mansions and upscale houses, put on the uniforms and go into battle.

We should demand that it's done the old-fashioned way. Not by bombing from tens of thousands of feet some innocent civilians, but by the ground offensive, where everyone has similar chances and where only those who are the most determined and brave will win.

If the "freedom," "democracy," but above all "free" trade, "open" markets and economic dominance are so sacred to our elites, let them fight for it. Let neo-cons and market fundamentalists form their own battalions and platoons. Let them train for the invasions in filthy ditches. Let them "spill their blood" for it. And let them also say: "those who are willing to join are welcome; those who want to leave are welcome to do so as well." If we would succeed in those demands, if participation of the elites in any invasion would become obligatory, it would lead to one and only result: permanent peace on earth.

Until we succeed though, let's not ridicule al-Sadr, a man from the city of Najaf, who is not obliging anyone to follow him, but is ready to defend his city even if he has to do it alone. Right or wrong, his behavior is more honorable and brave than the behavior of those who are throwing other people onto bloody battlefields all over the world, while risking nothing themselves.

August, 2004

Defending Venezuela

Those of us who lived and worked in Latin America were glued to television sets and computer monitors, following the outcome of a referendum in Venezuela, organized by the right wing opposition supported by the United States. Those of us who believe in progress, decency and equality rejoiced. Hugo Chavez, President and reformist, survived again, was endorsed by 58 percent of Venezuelan voters who had lined up for hours in front of the polling stations all over their huge and diverse country.

For years, Mr. Chavez defended those who were defenseless, facing tremendous pressure from the opposition, surviving blackmail, lies, a military coup backed by the US, strikes organized by right wing trade unions and business elites. He never backed away from his goal – helping the great majority of miserably poor citizens of his oil rich nation.

Venezuela voted and more than half of the people sent a clear message to their democratically elected President: "Stay!"

The vote itself was proof of civic maturity and enormous courage. Who could ever forget the elections in Nicaragua that followed the murderous actions committed by the CIA-backed Contras? There, the Sandinistas "lost," despite the support they were enjoying from the majority of the Nicaraguan people who were exhausted, hoping that the violence and terror by the Contras would stop if they voted the Sandinista leader Daniel Ortega out of power.

Mr. Chavez and his government survived every imaginable threat, refusing to yield to The Monroe Doctrine and to the danger of the "Chilean scenario." As occurred in the early 1970's in Chile, the powerful elites in Venezuela unleashed economic blackmail and a tremendous propaganda campaign, accusing Mr. Chavez of dictatorial tendencies and spreading outright lies about his political and economic motives. They contaminated their nation with uncertainty, fear and economic chaos.

Two years ago, elites brought the Venezuelan economy almost to its knees, then blamed Chavez for everything from declining GDP to increased violence on the streets of Caracas. The press and mass media, mainly owned by white right-wing businessmen, concentrated their efforts on defaming the President and his programs designed to help the poor (mainly black or indigenous).

During my last visit to Caracas I spoke to several journalists who complained about the same thing: "We support Chavez but can't put it in writing if we want to retain our jobs."

Chavez let them bark, concentrating instead on how to pull his country out of crisis and educate, cure and feed the poor. He also traveled the world (as the President of OPEC), negotiating fair prices for oil and trying to convince poor nations to unite and defend their own interests against the designs of the handful of rich countries.

Why is Hugo Chavez hated so much by the elites? The answer is simple: He is not one of them. He is not white and he is not rich. He never belonged to the small and exclusive club of the unimaginably corrupt political and economic hierarchy that bled the nation for decades. He forced the rich and their companies (including the international ones) to pay taxes.

In the past, Venezuelan politicians and big business negotiated huge international loans, easily accessible because of the country's oil reserves. Loans were intended for improvements of infrastructure, medical care and education, as well as for social development. Most of the money was stolen, disappeared, left the country in the pockets of corrupt elites. Then the Venezuelan poor and lower middle class were presented with the bill.

Chavez came up with the plan to break latifundias and distribute (mainly unused) land among the landless and poor peasants. By then, elites realized that he meant business, that his words were not empty rhetoric. In order to preserve their privileges, they united their forces against his government.

The US was a logical ally of those who dreamed about deposing Mr. Chavez. Washington disliked the progressive President from the very beginning, accusing him of talking to the "enemies" (to Libyan and Iraqi leaders) disapproving of his choice of Mr. Castro of Cuba as his personal friend (Venezuela helps Cuba by providing cheap oil).

Attempts to help the Venezuelan poor were also seen by the US as subversive and dangerous, threatening to spread all over Latin America and the rest of the developing world. So were his statements that Venezuela doesn't need huge foreign investment; instead it needs solid and permanent (not speculative) investment that would help the country develop and fight poverty.

The United States and Venezuelan elites repeatedly tried and failed to unseat Mr. Chavez. He survived one coup attempt, elections, referendums and past hard economic times (presently, the Venezuelan economy is growing rapidly). After the August 2004 referendum, there can be no doubt that he remains the democratically elected and supported (by the majority) President of Venezuela.

That's wonderful and definitely a cause for celebration! But the hard question still remains: What will happen next and how can Mr. Chavez be helped by those who believe that he is one of the last hopes for genuine and progressive reforms in Latin America and the entire developing world?

Opposition in Venezuela is tremendously powerful, well organized and united. It's ready to defend its privileges, its dominant position in the society, its luxury cars, villas, golf-courses and right to squeeze every penny from the poor majority. It still will be able to count on support from the North and many Latin American countries (in fact from the majority of them, especially those that treat their own indigenous and black citizens with contempt and arrogance); it still owns almost all the large businesses, most of the land

and almost all important television channels and daily and weekly newspapers. In the past, all efforts by progressive people of the world failed to prevent the destruction of Nicaragua and Chile. It also failed to stop terrorist attacks against Cuba, not to speak of the embargo. In order to survive and succeed, Venezuela will have to rely on much more than just the support of two or three forward-looking governments on its continent.

Every effort has to be made to support its leader and reforms. If Mr. Chavez fails, the greatest hope for social justice, decency and democracy for all may disappear from Latin America with easily imaginable and terrible consequences for the millions of dispossessed and desperate poor.

August, 2004

Indonesia Teaching France About Freedom?

In December 2003, in an attempt to "reaffirm separation of religions and state," a presidential panel decided that France should ban Islamic head scarves, as well as other "obvious religious and political symbols" from the public schools. On February 10, 2004, the French National Assembly voted (494 in favor, 36 against and 31 abstentions) to convert the decision into a law.

Mainstream politicians supported the decision but so did the right wing, many left-wing parties and organizations, as well as women's rights groups. Around the time when the decision was made, *The Economist* ran a survey indicating that while the majority of European Muslims opposed banning head scarves, most of them were men. The majority of Muslim women living in France expressed their support for the ban.

There were demonstrations in France and in other countries across Europe accusing the French government of discriminatory measures against its substantial Muslim minority. But France stood firm, defending its decision on the basis of historical secularism and separation of church and state.

One group that had hardly been surveyed was that of young Muslim girls living in France. Were they in favor of or against the head scarf ban? Were they forced to wear hijab or had a decision been made for them by their families? Had they freely chosen their faith?

Working in Indonesia, the most populous Muslim nation on earth, I surveyed several women when preparing the story on head scarves for a European magazine. One of the questions I asked was whether they supported the decision made in France. Answers were almost unanimous: every woman expressed outrage over the ban. Statements ranged from: "people should be allowed to express their religious beliefs" to "Indonesia could teach France about freedom."

But again, nobody mentioned the young girls.

So how would Indonesia fare in comparison with France when it comes to religious freedom?

On paper, Indonesia is a secular country, but it's illegal not to have a religion there. In fact, only a handful of religions are "allowed." Religion has to be engraved in identity cards; there is no option such as "other" or "no religion." The family determines what religion a child should belong to from birth.

After the US-sponsored coup in 1965 (that deposed the progressive president Sukarno, who opposed Western colonialism and imperialism), brutal massacres destroyed the Indonesian left. Members of the Communist Party were massacred or sent to jail. One of the main executors of the slaughter was NU – an enormous Islamic organization that held grudges against the left for earlier attempts to expropriate large land-holdings and distribute them among landless peasants. The Communist Party had been banned and so had all progressive ideas. In Suharto's Indonesia, not to have a religion was synonymous with being an atheist, a Marxist and therefore, an outlaw.

Tens of thousands of families lived in fear. Since most Indonesian extended families consist of tens and even hundreds of members, almost each and every one of them had some "skeleton in the closet" – someone who used to be involved in progressive unions or had been a member of the Communist Party.

One way to avoid persecution and to survive in the climate of fascist oppression was to show nationalist and religious zeal. One way to demonstrate that the family had broken with its "shameful past" was to turn its members into pious Muslims, to indoctrinate children, to make them comply with an increasingly conservative mainstream. While the majority of Indonesian society before 1965 had been secular and extremely relaxed about practical aspects or religion, in Suharto's era Indonesia accepted a large scale of conservative elements of Islam, influenced by Saudi Wahabism.

Religion brought full compliance and compliance was exactly what Suharto and his military cronies demanded. Head scarves became a normal occurrence, even among middle class, highly educated women. Mosques began broadcasting entire prayers over loudspeakers (a move hardly describable as tolerant toward members of other religions living in the same neighborhood), something unthinkable even in the Middle Eastern countries where only a call for prayer is audible. As the social system collapsed, mosques (often funded by conservative religious streams in the Middle East) became the only places where the poor and desperate could receive at least some meager help. Of course, there was a price-tag attached.

Now, it is not unusual to see girls, as young as five, walk down the dusty streets of the cities and villages fully covered, from head to toe. The number of segregated religious schools are on the increase. Can these girls choose whether to wear a head scarf or not?

Chances are that these girls will never have a chance to encounter alternative ideas. They will not read Hegel, Emmanuel Kant, Descartes, Sartre or, God forbid, Marx. Evolution theory will be mentioned at schools but immediately discounted. The fact that the biggest single group of people on this planet has no religion at all will be hidden from them. They will be "spared" any critical views offered by liberation Islam, too. They will never learn how to question and how to doubt. But they will be convinced that they actually opted freely for the head scarf, as they will believe that they are religious by their free choice. And this is Indonesia; a country often described as "moderate" and fairly "secular."

Once a member of a religion, it is basically impossible to escape. Society puts enormous pressures on its members and so do the families; especially on children and above all, girls, who are expected to marry as virgins, be fully obedient to their parents, are forced to pray from a very early age, memorize entire passages of scripture, are banned from cohabitation with their boyfriend once they grow up, and receive only one third of the inheritance.

"Exit from religion" in Indonesia is illegal, unless one converts to another faith. A family whose member decides to abandon his or her faith would be almost certainly socially ruined, ridiculed and scrutinized. It is impossible to imagine a person visiting his or her family during the month of Ramadan proudly announcing: "I decided to abandon my faith; I don't think I believe in any of this, anymore, so while you are going to the field, I'm going to do some shopping or search for a place to have a beer." This person would be immediately disowned, excommunicated, damned. There is only one choice – to have a religion and to conform.

In the ideally secular world, a child would be exposed to all views, to all religions and non-religious concepts. He or she would not be indoctrinated from childhood but instead, it would be explained to him or her, thoroughly, that there are many ways to understand our existence, our place in the world. When reaching a certain age, a young person would freely decide which religion to choose or whether to become an atheist or agnostic.

All of us are products of our environment, growing up in different parts of the world, influenced by distinctive ideas and concepts. Ideal concepts could, of course, not be fully implemented. And it's not only about religion (almost all of us, growing up in the West have to fight against indoctrination by market fundamentalism and by the superiority complex often pushed on us from behind grand words and slogans). But there should be an attempt to expose children to a variety of worldviews and to shelter them from one-sided indoctrination, offering them an entire range of different options on how to see and understand the world.

There should definitely be religious freedom in every decent society, and children should be protected. The question is: can a child truly decide that he or she is religious and consciously decide to wear symbols of his or her faith? Or is she simply conforming to her family's decision? Can a twelve year old girl truly be a staunch Marxist or free-marketer? Can she be a true Christian or Muslim? Shouldn't she be given some time, before she chooses labeling herself? Shouldn't secular society guarantee that she receive that time? Would it be, for instance, normal for an eleven year old girl to come to school with a T-shirt proclaiming "down with the God," or "Socialism or Death"?

France is again facing a tremendous philosophical and moral dilemma. Its decision to ban head scarves in public schools should not only be judged: it should trigger intensive and open discussion about how children worldwide are being indoctrinated (and again, not only by religions but also by consumerism, media and advertising) and how they can be protected. So far, there is not one single country that has succeeded in guaranteeing true secularity, offering equally all-important ideas of humanity to its children. Judged by its track record of the last 40 years, Indonesia could hardly be considered as a guiding light for France or any other society.

There are no easy answers and no easy solutions, but the issue is one of the most essential in today's world.

October, 2004

Are We Alone, Arundhati Roy?

Two years ago we met in the coffee shop of Park Hotel in Delhi. What was supposed to be a short encounter became a few hours long heated discussion about literature and events of September 11th. Arundhati was about to depart India for the US where she was invited to speak. I suggested that September 11 should not be just remembered as an anniversary of attacks against the World Trade Center and the Pentagon; it should be mourned as the day when, in 1973, the Chilean military sponsored by the US government and private companies destroyed one of the oldest democracies on earth.

We discussed politics and we discussed mounting problems in India, but we also talked about the state of literature, a topic about which we both felt passionate. We agreed that almost all great modern writers seemed to be in a lethargic sleep or too frightened to address important global issues. Or maybe there were almost no great writers left.

Philosophy, politics, social criticism and vision were replaced by frivolous, entertaining plots. The pitiful state of today's world, its disparities and scandalous post-colonial arrangement topped the list of some of the issues hardly discussed on the pages of contemporary novels. Fiction had become politically and socially detached and therefore historically and morally irrelevant. Instead of aiming at retaining their status as "the conscience of society," most writers opted for much more modest goals, turning themselves into entertainers and showbiz figures.

Great nonfiction writers were still around, writing brilliant books in the West, in India, and in Latin America, but the novel, a literary form so dear to both of us, seemed to be finished, sold out and stained by apparent – although somehow hesitant – collaboration with the business and commercial interests of those who were ruling our societies.

We parted in front of my hotel. I gave her a gift – a silk scarf from Vietnam – she gave me a hug, then entered her little beat-up car and drove away. I waved for a while, standing on the pavement, overwhelmed with absolute certainty that I had just parted with one of the bravest writers of our time.

Since then I have not had a chance to meet her again, but while working in the South Pacific I came across an issue of the Australian magazine *The Bulletin*, which carried a long article on Arundhati Roy by Jennifer Byrne. "...I'm actually a writer, and this is what writers do and have done through centuries – commenting on the societies in which they live. But now because writing and literature has become a kind of quote unquote commercial activity, it's dumbed them down like nothing ever has before, so we are supposed to be some kind of court entertainers."

Ms. Byrne asked whether there was really such a tradition, or was she (Roy) just being wishful? "Yeah, there was," answered Arundhati Roy. "Who were Sartre and George Orwell? And today it's reduced to something almost like toys, not even rigorous in your analysis. I mean who are the big writers today who have taken on what is huge in the world? Very few – unless they are on the other side. Like V.S. Naipaul commenting the other day that Saudi Arabia and Iran should be destroyed."

How could one disagree with Arundhati Roy? Of course, such a tradition existed for centuries, helping humanity move forward. The greatest writers stood at the vanguard of the struggle against racism, colonialism, and imperialism. They were promoting social justice, fought for changes. Romaine Rolland, Anatole France, Emile Zola, and Maxim Gorky placed themselves on the side of exploited, enslaved human beings, demanding immediate change, even revolution.

J. B. Shaw – probably the greatest modern British playwright consistently ridiculed the entire capitalist dogma, and his German counterpart – Bertold Brecht – openly called to arms against it.

There was an entire generation of outstanding novelists and thinkers in post-war France: Jean-Paul Sartre, Albert Camus, and Simone de Beauvoir to name just a few. All three ware active members of anti-fascist resistance, all three condemned the post-war arrangement of the world. In those days, philosophers and writers were not confined to the university campuses: when Sartre was addressing workers at a Renault factory, his speeches drew to the premises hundreds of thousands of men and women who, by the way, had no problem understanding what he was talking about!

There were great novelists like Andre Malroux, Ernest Hemingway, and Saint-Exupery (author of the famous philosophical book for children and adults – "Little Prince"), writers who fought in wars, engaging themselves not only by words but also by deeds. And their books were then selling millions of copies, despite the complex and often controversial topics they were addressing.

In the United States, Richard Wright shocked his readers all over the world with the novel "Native Son," a damning, powerful and honest account of racism and discrimination of African Americans. A few decades later, Joseph Heller described the insanity of the war (Catch-22) and later the hypocrisy of corporate America (Good as Gold).

Latin America offered some of the greatest novelists of the 20th century: Carlos Fuentes, Alejo Carpentier, Gabriel Garcia Marquez, and Manuel Puig from the left, as well as Jorge Borges and Maria Vargas Llosa from the other side of the political spectrum. In Africa, Chinua Achebe described the destruction of local cultures by colonialism in his novel "Things Fall Apart," while Indonesian author Pramoedya Ananta Toer defined brilliantly the painful process of the birth of the young nation and its horrific downfall after the fascist coup in 1965.

These are just a few examples from the past, but the list is endless. The fact is that almost all great literature since ancient Greece has dealt with the most important issues facing humanity: from Homer to Victor Hugo to Franz Kafka to Albert Camus. That modern writers are stubbornly refusing to address serious problems of the world is a disturbing anomaly, an exception from the historic rule, proof that something has gone terribly wrong, even in the societies that proudly claim their intellectual brilliance. The history of literature simply doesn't know any other period like this!

The world is full of tremendous stories. Global market fundamentalism and neo-conservative culture are overthrowing all democratic principals for which humanity has fought for centuries. Millions of people are dying having no access to medicine, while pharmaceutical conglomerates (backed by the governments of rich countries) are blocking developing nations from producing cheap drugs that would save their men, women, and children.

Humanity is experiencing new colonial wars as well as religious and business extremism. Small island nations may soon disappear due to global warming. The gap between rich and poor nations is growing. Quality of life in the United States is declining, while Europe is dismantling its welfare system. There is confusion and dissatisfaction in many developed countries, and there is anger and growing resentment toward the rich world in most of the desperate nations. In many poor places, conservative forms of religions are dangerously filling the gap left after the systematic destruction of social movements and progressive governments.

Great stories are plentiful: they are offering themselves in the desperate shantytowns of Lima and Jakarta; in the fast-food restaurants and sweatshops in the US where exploited men, women, and children are laboring at minimum wages; in the battlefields of the Middle East, Southeast Asia, and Africa; in indigenous huts of Mexico, Bolivia, and Guatemala; as well as in the small island nations of the

South Pacific that are slowly but irreversibly disappearing from the face of the earth.

These are stories of monumental proportions, honest and good stories, stories that can terrify while evoking compassion; stories that can call for action – stories that the novel as a form is capable of telling.

If there is no lack of great stories, is there a lack of great writers? Or have they been silenced, sidelined and marginalized? Have they been broken and starved, or maybe forced to accept some regular job that allows them to survive but prevents them from writing? Have they sold out, writing romance novels and self improvement books, producing hundreds of pages describing their erections, coming of age, getting old or trying to solve some fictitious criminal plot?

There are still some great novelists left; not many, but there are. Jose Saramago, Arundhati Roy, Tariq Ali, even Salman Rushdie who is presently levitating in some strange realm while we, down here, are hoping that he may soon land again on the progressive side of the barricade. There is still Gunter Grass and Garcia Marquez.

But there is also an acute lack of young writers, angry and daring, determined to change the world and to offer new alternatives to the stale intellectual swamp created by market/business fundamentalism and its faithful servant – the cheap, thought-destroying entertainment industry that is lately swallowing almost all major publishing houses and independent bookstores.

It is easy and correct to a certain degree to say that it's now almost impossible to write a great novel against the establishment, while expecting it to be published and promoted. The media and publishing houses are far from being independent. Most of them are part of large companies which are hardly ecstatic about printing books dangerous to their own interests and designs.

But the process of writing should never be fully influenced by mercantile considerations. The writer is a storyteller, an artist, a witness, a judge and a thinker. He or she leaves important testimony about a particular time and puts on record what others would often not even dare to pronounce. The financial reward is important (as reward for any hard work should be), but longing for it must never influence the choice of the subject or style in which the book is written. If it does, the result is almost certainly rubbish.

I'm a novelist, and I believe that novel is the most complete artistic form capable of describing reality, the state of the world, the grievances and hopes of the people. I also believe that it should never aim at anything less than that.

My latest book *Point of No Return* shows the world through the eyes of war correspondents, visiting places that are rarely covered by the dominant media, offering provocative points of view that are hardly acceptable to the present world of entertainment which now includes most of the traditional publishing houses. But writing itself, writing the truth is a privilege and joy. It is worth any inconvenience, any hardship.

I suspect that Arundhati Roy would agree with my views. But are we becoming an endangered, almost extinct species? Are serious topics going to be openly ridiculed and described as outdated? Is it already happening? Are readers going to accept this approach? Are we really expected to become entertainers, clowns, even liars? Are we supposed to forget about all those great novels written in the past?

Or are we going to swim with all our strength against the powerful (main)stream?

I don't think we have much choice. If we float, if we allow ourselves to be carried by this current, we will end up in the land of irrelevance, oblivion, and shame.

November, 2004

Republicans Won - The Rest Of The World Lost

It was late at night and I had been glued to the screen of the television set in Apia, the tiny capital of Samoa. The signal of the BBC World kept disappearing, despite all the gadgets that were supposed to reinforce it – the satellite dish and something called the outside booster. As the night was journeying into the dawn, more parts of the map of the United States were being covered by the color red. Blue was at the extreme geographical edges – Northeast and West – and with some little spots in the middle. Red seemed to be everywhere else.

Then another red color appeared – this time that of the rising sun – behind the window, illuminating the tranquil majesty of open ocean, the white edges of waves breaking over the tips of coral, the lush greenery of tropical vegetation.

For just a short moment I played with the thought that what was happening thousands of miles away in my country was irrelevant, compared to the enormity of nature. But then why were my eyes watering?

I wrote an email to Michael Albert. He said that at that moment he simply couldn't write. I tried to write myself, but couldn't, either. I went to the terrace and smoked. Surprisingly, I wasn't thinking about Ohio and Wisconsin, not even about New York. I tried to remember war zones that I had to cover for many years, and about places that were trying to cope with the devastation brought about by the business interests of my country and by the governments that were serving them.

I thought about rice fields dotted with unexploded mines in Vietnam and Laos, about the craters left after the carpet bombing of Cambodia, about all the hopes and reason destroyed after 1965 in Indonesia, about the people of East Timor, still starving years after the end of the occupation supported by our government.

I thought about Cuba enduring a senseless and sadistic embargo, about the grayness and despair of Gaza City, about starvation that I had witnessed in Northern Nicaragua and across the border in Honduras.

I wondered how many places would soon be added to the list of our client states, would be defined as solid and trustworthy democracies, while the lives of their people would be reduced to a survival minimum, a subsistent existence with no hope and no future. How many millions of men, women and children would have to become direct slaves of our market fundamentalism and geopolitical interests?

As Bush was declaring his victory, almost all world markets went up, celebrating his survival in their own predictable way, a fact that probably didn't surprise anybody. Kerry suggested that it was time for healing, later returning to his bedroom, catching up on sleep of which he had been deprived for several nights due to last minute campaigning. In his own way he lost, but he lost with style and dignity, falling no lower than the cushions of his comfortable bed.

Those who really lost were billions of people living all over the world on one or two dollars a day, in their metal shacks, bamboo huts, overcrowded housing projects, standing whole days at dangerous assembly lines, working in the fields of subsistence farming. With Kerry in the White House, they wouldn't particularly win either, but this way it was clear and obvious that they had squarely and patently lost.

Right after the election, the war in Iraq escalated, as if the US military planners felt that they had received a green light from the voters back home to continue massive bombing campaigns and assaults, causing casualties mainly among civilians.

During the next few days I read online tens of newspapers and magazines. Both left and right, they were analyzing elections, explaining the reasons behind Bush's survival in the White House and the Republicans' gains in Congress. There were those, including Greg Palast, who exposed irregularities in the election process. Some suggested there was outright fraud.

Others correctly pointed out that it was hard to speak about free and democratic elections in the climate of direct media manipulation, propaganda campaigns and selective information offered to the American public in regard to their nation and the rest of the world.

Some writers mentioned that 40 percent of the American people didn't bother to vote at all – a number higher than that which any of the candidates received.

This was all correct, but so was the fact that, for whatever reason, at least one half of those who decided to vote did give their support to George W. Bush. Reality can be explained and analyzed, but it can't be denied and the United States as a nation has to take full responsibility for the consequences which this election will bring.

Michael Albert (in his article "Tomorrow is a Long Time") correctly depicts similarities between this election and the one in 1972, when Richard Nixon won a landslide victory and a second term in office.

But in 1972, when the American public elected a major crook as President of the mightiest nation, the world was polarized.

In 2004, there is no "second power" and the most important international organization – the United Nations – has been already humiliated and several times described as "irrelevant." There is almost nothing left of the Social Democratic, Labor and Socialist parties in Western and Central Europe, except their names.

Russia has become an uneasy ally of the US; the Chilean alternative was destroyed more than 30 years ago; the Central American progressive movements were ruined and the several governments still ready to resist market dictatorship (that of Chavez, for instance) are under constant pressure, hardly surviving our direct and indirect assaults and interventions.

At present, there is only one political and military superpower and American voters elected a man who will be representing it (although not really leading it, because even the government is lately becoming irrelevant, taking a dictate from the big business interests) for the next four years.

It is uncomfortable, but it has to be pronounced: President Bush will be representing the interests of a small group of elites at home and abroad – the unopposed and "unbalanced" power (a potential mightiness of which even the founding fathers never dared to predict) that now controls much of the entire world. Disparities will grow and every attempt to form dissent will be crushed, especially in the poor and far away countries. The major media will continue to play its servile role, trying to convince its readers and viewers that the world still has plenty of free choices.

If Kerry were elected, he would not have been able or willing to stop this process. But at least it could have been comforting and reassuring if the majority of American voters would have been able to identify and reject a candidate of market and religious fundamentalism. It didn't happen and the pace of "changes" will now accelerate at home and abroad.

Those changes will be more dramatic and brutal in the poor countries (the great majority of the world) than at home. There, many people will hold us – voters and citizens of the United States – responsible for the impact these elections will have on their lives. They see results, not the nuances. As far as they are concerned, we had a chance to change or to reverse the course and we didn't do it. We have chosen the most extreme one of the bunch.

Many of us, who are now mourning over the results of the election, know how complex the issue is. But from the outside, it all seems much simpler. The mightiest nation on earth has voted. Four more years of this government is what it has selected. Our voters had a choice. Those outside our national boundaries – those who will have to be subservient to our government and economic interests – had no choice at all.

During the next four years, those of us who are opposing the present system will have to fight on behalf of our own nation and also on behalf of those billions all over the world who were not allowed to cast a vote in our election but whose lives will be further ruined by its results.

November, 2004

Aceh Goes To Heaven!

Resting in a comfortable seat of a super-express speeding toward northern Japan, I was admiring the snow-covered beauty of the rural countryside behind the window. It was getting dark and the wheels of the train were gently drumming against the rails in a monotonous and reassuring rhythm. The world seemed harmonious and safe.

Then suddenly my eyes caught sight of the letters of a news bulletin passing through the digital display above the door. A strong earthquake had shaken northern Sumatra. There were dozens of casualties. Just that – no further information was provided. I checked the news, one hour later, on the internet in my hotel in Sendai. It seemed that hundreds of people had lost their lives in Indonesia, Sri Lanka, India and Thailand. An earthquake off the coast of Aceh, reaching a magnitude of 9 on the Richter scale, was followed by a tsunami – a monstrous 10 meters high tidal wave – which crashed mercilessly and with unimaginable force against the shores of several unfortunate countries.

In the next few days the number of victims grew to thousands, then to tens of thousands. Whole villages, entire towns disappeared from the map. Hundreds of thousands of refugees hit what was left of the roads, but roads were leading nowhere; bridges were washed away, floods were fragmenting the entire North of Sumatra Island. Electricity and water supply had collapsed (limited and unreliable everywhere in Indonesia even before the disaster); there was no food, no blood for the injured and no medicine. There was no reliable information either, since the foreign press was banned from traveling to the province, "for its own safety."

The Army – a tremendous contingent of it based in the province in order to suppress insurgency – did close to nothing. It was ordered to clean corpses and it cleaned some, but it otherwise showed no initiative, leaving the desperate population with almost no help.

The government did close to nothing. Instead of ordering special military units to travel immediately to the province, instead of using hundreds of military helicopters and aircraft in order to supply food and medicine, instead of ordering all seaworthy vessels to the area of disaster, the President of Indonesia urged the citizens to "scale down New Year's celebrations and pray instead."

Huge transport planes were sitting on runways all over Java, waiting for the order to take off – an order which never arrived.

Instead of employing professionals trained to cope with emergency situations, vice president Jusuf Kalla used military planes and commercial aircraft in order to shuttle

Muslim militants (they called themselves "volunteers") from *Majelis Mujahedeen Indonesia* and *Islamic Defenders Front* (Front Pembela Muslim – better known as its acronym FPI – a militant Muslim group from Jakarta devoted to enforcing Islamic law against drinking, gambling and prostitution), a fact later reported by *The New York Times*. Then Laskar Jihad, one of the most militant Muslim groups in Southeast Asia made inroads into the province. Hundreds of Christians, mainly of Chinese origin, were forced to flee Aceh.

The presence of "volunteers" – directly sponsored by the government – had one main purpose: to secure Indonesian and religious order (already the strictest in entire Indonesia) in the province which had been fighting for independence for almost thirty years, at enormous cost. Practically speaking, these untrained urbanites were only taking precious space in scarce flights to the province, although the propaganda machine fired out stories about how some of them single-handedly managed to restore electric supplies and telecommunications in Banda Aceh.

And the dead kept mounting, diseases spread, hunger began to kill those who had miraculously survived the brutality of nature.

At one point refusal to help Aceh began to look like vengeance killing by the government and the military. Then Aceh suddenly appeared in the spotlight of interest of the international community and after some hesitation, the government "benevolently" allowed foreign aid and some international press agencies to enter the province.

Results were almost immediate. International organizations and foreign military flew in and began building infrastructure from scratch. Not rebuilding it – there was not much in terms of social infrastructure even before the tsunami – but constructing provisory hospitals, food supply centers, shelters for the homeless for the first time. It was not enough, but it was at least something; definitely more than the state had done in the last three decades about investment in social infrastructure.

While this was happening, the Indonesian government was bragging that disaster is not going to jeopardize predicted economic growth for year 2005 (the lowest in the region even before tsunami).

The finance Minister openly declared that Indonesia expects foreigners to rebuild the area, while the state diverts no substantial funds from its own coffers. He was also quick to point out that vital oil production (the main reason for the occupation and the main income of the province – basically controlled by foreign multinationals, after corrupt deals signed by Suharto's government a few decades ago) suffered only a minor setback, although some inside reports suggest the contrary.

The government also suggested that Aceh is an outskirt of Indonesia; therefore its plight will have no major impact on the economy. In fact, it argued with no scruples, Indonesia could benefit, because it may attract thousands of tourists who would avoid the damaged holiday resorts in Thailand.

To put the situation into perspective, the social system in Indonesia collapsed during the years when Suharto, supported by the West, fully controlled the political and economic life of Indonesia. This was also a period when Indonesians went through rigorous religious indoctrination which was supposed to reinforce the culture of obedience, which in turn served the regime.

Almost all public services were privatized; the quality of education nose-dived; and life expectancy stagnated at around 64 years (one of the lowest in the region). Indonesia has, per capita, one of the highest numbers of orphans anywhere in the world and one of the worst records of child prostitution in the region. The poor have no safety net and justice is for sale. Indonesia, according to "Transparency International," is one of the most corrupt nations on earth.

The Indonesian military was involved in the massacre of Sukarno's supporters after the coup in 1965 (up to 3 million people were butchered in a matter of months); it led the genocidal war in East Timor (one of the most horrific barbarities of the 20th century, happily applauded by the West), and was responsible for gross human rights violations in Papua, Ambon, Aceh and elsewhere. It was and still is much better trained in raping and torturing civilians than in any sort of humanitarian assistance.

This compassionless, paralyzed and morally corrupt society was now facing one of the most terrible natural disasters in human history. Government officials and their business associates smelled a tremendous influx of foreign aid, which could, if unchecked, easily meet the same fate as the money from former foreign loans originally intended for development, infrastructure and social programs but which disappeared in the deep pockets of elites, never reaching the impoverished majority of Indonesian people.

As foreign governments were trying to outdo each other in pledging hundreds of millions of dollars for reconstruction of disaster stricken areas, Indonesian officials and military on the ground in Aceh were openly sabotaging relief efforts.

Food and medicine were piling up in Medan and Banda Aceh, while almost no help was reaching desperate communities. A chartered Boeing 737 hit a buffalo after landing, shutting down for hours the only runway in then the only functioning airport in entire Aceh. Apparently it was not worth assigning the military to guard this vital lifeline. But was it really an accident?

"One of the consequences of the lack of distribution of aid and medical assistance to several refugee camps has been the death of many refugees, especially women and children," says Yulia Evina Bhara from SEGERA (Alliance-Solidarity Movement For the People of Aceh). "This has occurred in Mata Le, Ulee Kareng, and a large part of Pidie and Aceh Jeumpa.... It is evident that the government has not taken any cooperative steps in terms of allowing easy access to areas in which aid needs to be distributed. If this continues to be the case, it means that the government is effectively disregarding the much needed humanitarian solidarity..."

Shortly after tsunami hit the coast, GAM (Free Aceh Movement) declared a ceasefire. A few days later there were reports that the Indonesian military continued with its operations. Sporadic exchanges of fire erupted in several places in Aceh. With no shame and no hesitation, the President of Indonesia began accusing GAM of breaking the ceasefire.

The foreign major press (traditionally friendly to the post-1965 Indonesian regime), which initially concentrated its coverage strictly on the disaster itself and later on the foreign relief operations, began asking some uncomfortable questions. Although still omitting information concerning the horrific human rights record of Indonesian state, it couldn't fully ignore the voices of Acehnese people who were accusing the government of sabotaging relief operations.

Sharp criticism of Indonesian government and military also came from foreign aid workers.

That seemed to be unacceptable to the establishment. On January 9th, the government began tightening restrictions on the movement of foreigners in the province. Reuters reported that on the 11th of January all goodwill vanished. Indonesia restricted foreign aid workers to two large cities because of "militant threats."

The Indonesian army chief – General Endriartono Sutarto – declared that GAM might soon attack foreign aid workers or troops in Aceh. All aid agencies and NGOs operating in the province were urged to provide a full list of their staff.

GAM responded by denying all accusations made by the government, claiming that it never intended to cause harm to those who came to help, be it foreigners or locals. Foreigners operating in Aceh confirmed that they felt no threat from the independence movement.

A crackdown on independent sources of information by the Indonesian state is becoming inevitable. As in East Timor, Papua and Aceh (before the disaster) it will be done under the cover of "protecting" lives of the foreigners. The question is what will happen to the Acehnese people afterwards. Even now, several members of Indonesian NGOs claim that the government actions (or more precisely – inaction) are responsible for at least 50 thousand out of 100 thousand known victims of the disaster.

Is Aceh going to become another East Timor? Is the present situation just a result of impotence and the incapability of the government, military and the whole system, or of something much more sinister? Is it revenge; an extermination campaign designed to break and secure this economically vital province?

The Acehnese are proud and tough people. When Javanese elites were selling their country to foreigners, when most of the islands of today's Indonesia were accepting the presence of Dutch colonizers, Aceh fought bitterly for independence. "Under the Dutch, Java used to send assassins to break Aceh," said Pramoedya Ananta Toer, the greatest Indonesian writer and intellectual father of the Indonesian state. "We have so much to learn from them!"

Recently, exploited by foreign multinational companies and by new Javanese elites, the people of Aceh began to fight again, against all odds. This time they fought against the Indonesian state – against one of the largest military forces on earth. 10 thousand men, women and children have died in almost three decades of the conflict; maybe much more.

One of the "profound" religious interpretations of this disaster in Indonesia was that God punished the people of Aceh for fighting for their independence. The official media even managed to find some Acehnese who declared it on the record. "If we don't stop fighting, we'll all go to hell."

Those who always suspected that there are no eternal flames, those who respect human life above anything else always knew that Aceh had already been going through a hell for many years. But "hell is the others" – those who fight innocent civilians, those who torture, those who are blocking help from the suffering people in the moment of tremendous need and catastrophe.

If those who are using disaster and human suffering for their own political, economic and military goals are not stopped soon, the entire country of Indonesia may soon go to hell. Not to some hell depicted by religious books – but a real hell which is life in a society which has lost all basic moral human values; which allows a small minority of people to live a vulgar lavish life at the expense of tens of millions of those who are starving and desperate.

Aceh is bleeding and the worst may still be ahead. Those who are arriving in Aceh should know that they are not only entering a land devastated by a horrific natural disaster; they are entering a territory which has been brutalized and exploited for decades and which still is. It doesn't only need aid – it needs solidarity, protection and determined long-term help; and it needs it now! It needs a referendum and – if it decides to vote for it – freedom. Anything would be better than the present situation – from here Aceh can only go to heaven!

January, 2005

Aceh Abandoned - The Second Tsunami

There is no "Ground Zero" in Banda Aceh – no single point which can be defined as the epicenter of disaster. A tremendous wave leveled entire neighborhoods to the ground. Closer to the coast, what remains of the city has a striking resemblance to the old black and white photographs of Hiroshima after the devastating nuclear explosion.

Hundreds of mass-graves have not been covered.

People are cautiously returning, searching for bodies. In the neighborhood of Puekan Bada, the smell of decomposing flesh is unbearable. Bodies are everywhere, buried under the rubble and dead trees, or simply floating in the stale water. After one month in the water, bodies are unrecognizable. The flesh is almost gone; the hardened skin is tightly attached to the skeleton.

Bodies – some in yellow and blue plastic bags, others exposed to the sun – are resting on the bottom of deep pits. Heavy equipment: bulldozers, excavators, and trucks are idly parked just a few meters away. There seems to be no lack of machinery or fuel, but almost no organized effort to put it to use.

Jamaludin, a forty year old man, is searching through the rubble, machete in his hand. He lost almost all the members of his family. Now he sleeps in one of the refugee camps at night. "TNI (military) set up several camps in the area, but they abandoned us a few days later. The government sometimes delivers water, but it is not clean. Several people that I know have stomach infections; severe diarrhea."

He guides me through the rubble to the body bags. "We don't know what to do with them. We have no shovels ourselves, but according to the Muslim tradition, bodies have to be buried. Some gangs visit this area at night, burning the bodies with petrol. That's absolutely wrong, but there is nothing we can do – it's unsafe and horrifying to stay in this area at night!"

The government has declared that victims will not be allowed to rebuild their houses within 2 or 3 kilometers of the coast. Those who survived the tsunami are supposed to be relocated ("for safety reasons"), but no concrete plans have yet been presented. Local people believe that the government and big businesses are planning a "land-grab" in potentially lucrative areas close to the coast.

Mr. Syamsuddin, one of the former inhabitants of Lamteungoh village sums up the frustration of the local people: "The government tells us that we cannot return to our homes if they are closer than 2 kilometers from the coast. We all know that this is the best land. But the government and the businesses don't want to pay anything. They are just promising to relocate us. Once we are gone, they can develop this area into an industrial zone or build hotels, golf-courses, anything.... For them this is a great opportunity to make money; they are taking advantage of this disaster and our suffering. This is still our land! If they will compensate us fairly, we will accept. If not, we will stay and fight!"

According to Mr. Syafruddin – the coordinator of CARE ACEH, a local humanitarian NGO – the government is not planning to give any compensation to the victims of the tsunami. "They [the government] say that the refugees will be relocated, their houses rebuilt somewhere else, but no location has been designated so far, and there is no exact budget. Given the government's track-record, we are afraid that most of the funds will disappear. Care Aceh is advocating for the rebuilding of houses at their original location."

INADEQUATE RESPONSE

There is hardly any doubt that the government in Jakarta failed to respond promptly and adequately to the natural disaster which can only be described as one of the most devastating in human history.

Hours after the giant tidal wave killed more than 200,000 people, the government of Indonesia made no coordinated effort to launch a massive rescue and relief operation. Only six transport C-130 airplanes were mobilized and even these were not ordered to take off immediately (Banda Aceh airport was damaged, but not the one in Medan, from where the aid could have been transported by land).

Instead of declaring a national state of emergency and mobilizing private airliners and ships for relief operations in Aceh, the government advised the citizens to pray for the victims. Jusuf Kalla, the Vice-President and newly elected head of Golkar Party (the same political force which ruled the country during Suharto's dictatorship), decided to use precious space in C-130 planes to fly "volunteers" – his supporters from several religious movements like MMI/Majelis and FPI – for his own political goals.

Maulana Ibrahim, a youth leader from Aceh assessed the work of these volunteers: "We saw hundreds of volunteers coming to Aceh just days after the disaster. They arrived from Jakarta, Yogyakarta, and even Pontianak. Almost all of them were amateurs, unable to work in extreme conditions. They themselves were depressed and horrified, unable to lift the spirits of local victims. Some doctors couldn't handle these conditions and abandoned their post after two days. The government gave them no maps; they did not know where to go, did not know names of the districts.... Logistically, their presence was a total disaster."

Mr. Asraw, coordinator of PCC (People's Crises Center – arguably the most active humanitarian NGO in Aceh), described volunteers from Jakarta as: "people who complicated the situation even further. They were taking photographs of dead bodies, looking like tourists. Some volunteers were just government spies, although after the Martial Law, one would wonder why the government needed more of them.... My conclusion: most of the volunteers did close to nothing."

"It's not only that government forces did almost nothing," continues Mr. Asraw. "In many cases they were preventing aid from reaching the refugees. We know about corruption cases, like the one in PEMDA, district of Dewantara in North Aceh, where the local government, instead of giving urgently needed aid to refugees, passed it to the local military commander. Even here in Banda Aceh, the military was selling aid supplies through warungs (local shops). The PCC office had been visited by the military on several occasions – they were demanding food and water. They were very rude. Once, our worker asked them to fill out the papers – a normal procedure. Soldiers got angry and began kicking and destroying huge, and then so precious, bottles of water."

Almost all relief agencies working in the field agree that approximately 70 percent of the aid came from abroad. The locals are scared of the moment when the international community decides to pull out of Aceh. There is graffiti all over the province, asking in English: "Please help us!"

From the very start, the Indonesian government didn't try to hide the fact that helping Aceh was not on top of its agenda. Just a few days after the disaster, the Minister of Finance declared that the nation's economic growth would not be seriously affected, because Aceh is on the outskirts of Indonesia. He also noted that reconstruction efforts would be financed mainly from abroad.

Those who suffered were mostly poor Acehnese. Natural gas and oil production (controlled mainly by multinational companies) detected almost no disruption. "It's remarkable," commented Deddy Afidick – an executive of Exxon/Mobile, seated in his luxury villa – far away from disaster area – in Banda Aceh. "Our oil-fields suffered no damage. We can speak about zero damage! And the same goes for our friends at LNG – no destruction at all!"

"FIRST TSUNAMI" REVISITED

Away from the coastal areas of Aceh, there is no destruction. Roads pass through pristine countryside. Green fields, sleepy villages and high mountains in the distance. All this looks like a stereotypical image of earthly paradise taken straight from some tourist brochure. The only disturbance comes from armored police and military trucks, driven at head-breaking speed, pushing all other vehicles off the road.

But behind the facade of this pristine beauty, there are military and police checkpoints in every village. And in almost every house – misery and often hunger.

On the advice of one of the local NGOs, I drive to the area of Desa Siron, to the old village of Keureung Krung. All houses are traditional, made of wood. The entire village runs toward the car – to welcome me. I ask about the refugees. There are several families who managed to escape from the devastated areas on the coast.

"These children lost their families. Their relatives were swept away by the sea," explains an old woman with a wrinkled and exhausted face. "We received no aid from the government. There is nothing we can do; we went to Lambaro and talked to the government officials. They gave us nothing; they sent no people here. We were trying to talk to the District leaders, but he refused to see us. Nobody cares, especially the government. We need food, we need medicine; we need some help for children who experienced terrible trauma. We are so angry! People in this village are feeding us. They are the only ones willing to help, but they have almost nothing themselves!"

After some hesitation, a group of elders decides to approach me. They need to speak to me, they say. We enter a small, humble mosque and seat ourselves on the floor in a circle.

"You are the first journalist who ever came here," says the village chief. "Nobody ever visits this place; we are cut-off from the world. The military comes here several times a week, always at night. They torture us and they beat us; we feel humiliated and desperate. The military asks the same question: "Where is GAM (Free Aceh Movement)?" They give us no time to answer; they begin beating us, putting our head under the water until we can't breath. They even beat women. We heard that the military was supposed to help the Acehnese after the tsunami. But they do the same things to us now as they did before."

"They usually arrive at 3AM; four or six of them, riding Honda motorbikes. They are from "Pasukan Raider" ("Raider Troops"), but they have no name tags. All we know is that their leader's nickname is Ampah."

"Once I was tortured so brutally that I couldn't move for hours, afterwards. We are not brave to fight back – they have guns and we are not armed. And they seem to be drunk, or maybe insane. They torture our elders, even one blind man from this village. They just enjoy doing it! They shoot our animals, shooting cows with machineguns, point blank. They destroy houses and prevent us from tending to our rambutan trees, cucumber and rice fields.... They break our fences, so the wild animals can get in and domestic animals can escape."

"They killed almost 20 men around here, some 5 months ago. There was no battle, no confrontation. Only a few of those killed were members of GAM; the rest were just villagers – bystanders. We don't want the Indonesian military around here! We have had enough; we can't take it anymore! This is happening all over Aceh; not only in the villages here, but everywhere outside the major cities!"

"When GAM fighters come here, they never treat us like this. When they visit their family here, they always bring food with them. They always come alone – humbly. And they never carry guns when they come home. But the Indonesians? How can we ever make a deal with Indonesia? How can we even talk? They never listen to us. They just beat us; torture us before we can say anything! People here say that Aceh has been hit by the second tsunami. Our first tsunami was the imposition of Martial Law in May 2003!"

POSITION OF GAM

After some complicated security maneuvers (meeting local guides and exchanging passwords), I am taken to one of the military leaders of GAM – commander Nasir – who is in charge of the area of Banda Aceh and Aceh Besar. I have to climb a steep rocky mountain, before encountering two fully armed fighters, who escort me to their commander, a forty year old man with a mustache and firm handshake.

Although we are in the middle of the wilderness we take our shoes off, seating ourselves on a straw mat.

Peace talks between the Indonesian government and GAM just collapsed in Helsinki, Finland. The government refuses to even discuss the possibility of a referendum, fearing that the Acehnese people would overwhelmingly vote for independence, as people in East Timor did. When the bilateral talks between the two sides collapsed the last time, fighting erupted and countless lives were lost.

After the tsunami both the GAM and the government declared a ceasefire, but since then, the Indonesian government and the military has accused GAM of igniting a new wave of violence and has sent out a security warning to the members of the international community, active in Aceh.

Most of the foreign workers in Aceh discount such government warnings as baseless. GAM has said that it has never considered attacking foreigners. Instead it accuses the government and the military of taking advantage of the post-tsunami chaos to conduct military operations against them and the Acehnese civilians. By the end of January, the government declared that it was "forced to kill 120 GAM members."

"All this is just government propaganda," says commander Nasir. "After the tsunami we tried to help the Acehnese people. And we did help, before the arrival of the foreign aid workers, because the government did absolutely nothing. About the TNI killing 120 of our fighters – it is absolute nonsense. What happened is this: in Lamno, the army fired at people who came to search for their families after the tsunami, killing 5 civilians and 2 GAM members. We refused to return fire, since we had orders not to fight back."

I ask him about GAM's long-term strategy.

"We will fight for the freedom of Aceh and we will never give up, before it is achieved. We want full independence from Indonesia, but we will yield to the wishes of our people. If they opt for something less, we will have to accept. But first of all, the people have to be consulted: they should have a free referendum. Whatever their decision is, GAM will comply."

I ask commander Nasir whether GAM is a religious or a secular guerrilla force?

"We are definitely not a religious movement, although since this is Aceh, most of us are Muslims. We have no atheists and no Christians among our fighters, but we have many supporters who are Chinese or Christians. If any of them would choose to join us, we would have no problems accepting them. As for the ideology: we are training our fighters in the Acehnese ideology. It means that we give them the Acehnese identity, we teach them our language, our culture and our history."

Commander Nasir then continues to add, "I would like to thank the international community: Thank you! Thank you for coming here and helping our people. You don't have to worry about us. We will never harm you. We are grateful. Please stay as long as you can because once you leave, the suffering of the Acehnese will increase again."

THE TSUNAMI AS SEEN FROM BANDA ACEH AND JAKARTA

Although both Banda Aceh and Jakarta are in the same country, there is little knowledge in the capital about what really happened during and after the tragedy.

Indonesia is often incorrectly described by the dominant Western media as a "democratic country." In reality it is a post-dictatorial society, where big businesses, military and religious institutions still maintain an unchallenged grip on power and the local media is controlled by the business elites.

"There is a limit to what can be written about the military, for instance," explains the senior editor of one of the major magazines in Indonesia (he asked not to be identified). "And the same goes for the police. If we cross the line, we are risking our life and our magazine can be ruined."

"Most of the people get their news from television," explains an Indonesian TV reporter, who also prefers to remain anonymous. "While magazines can at least offer some criticism, television stations are much more limited. They can't be openly critical of the government, military and the police. The great majority of the Indonesian public never encounters direct criticism of the government's handling of the disaster in Aceh. People simply don't know. And, honestly, they don't care!"

Dissent is still brutally suppressed. Last year, an influential human rights activist and government critic, Munir, was poisoned on board the Indonesian airlines flight from Jakarta to Amsterdam. No thorough investigation has been conducted yet.

"Government Watch" coordinator and anti-corruption activist, Farid Faqih, was arrested in Aceh in January and still remains in jail, facing the ridiculous charges of stealing aid from the military-controlled warehouses. Mr. Faqih was brutally beaten by several members of the armed forces.

Vice-President Jusuf Kalla described the beating as a "misunderstanding," while Mr. Faqih still awaits a trial in jail.

At the end of January, an American journalist and filmmaker – William Nessen – was expelled for the second time from the country – this time for entering Indonesia illegally since he is apparently barred from the country. This is ironic given that Mr. Nessen entered the country openly, purchasing his visa upon arrival from the local officials.

This is just a short and an incomplete list of recent abuses against the critics of the system.

While the Acehnese people are outraged by the government's inefficient response to the disaster, viewers in Jakarta are bombarded by the state sponsored propaganda, describing the glorious deeds of its army and the volunteers. As a result, the majority of the Indonesians describe the government's response to the tsunami as somehow slow, but adequate (according to a poll run by METRO-TV).

There is no public outcry. No heads are rolling. The Indonesian media continues to show tremendous servility and discipline.

TRAUMA AND HOPELESNESS

Those who survived often gather with other victims, sharing their stories, grief and frustration. Some of them lost one or two relatives. Others lost everybody and everything.

Many survivors wander aimlessly through the rubble, others sit on what remains of their homes. There are people who prefer to be surrounded by their relatives and friends (if any survived); others choose to be alone. Most people are quiet; there are hardly any loud and evident displays of despair or sorrow.

"Some people cry, some don't," explains Ms. Laetitia de Schoutheete, a famous Belgian psychologist who joined the team of Doctors without Borders in Aceh. "Those people who survived are no longer sure about their future. Right now, they simply can't afford to cry or to grieve. The moment their security is guaranteed, the grief process will begin. But when it begins, it is very hard to predict what will happen."

For most of the surviving victims, the "guarantee of security" is still far away. There are almost no jobs in Aceh and the ones available pay meager salaries – too low to save anything in order to start a new life. Full days work of cleaning rubble in the city center pays only 30.000Rp – around $3.25. Tens of thousands of small family businesses have been lost, fishing boats destroyed. The government doesn't seem to have any sound plan for revitalization of the devastated area, although officially it has already moved to the "reconstruction stage." The United Nations now estimates that some 800,000 people in Aceh will have to be fed for a prolonged period of time – maybe for as long as two years.

Prices for basic food have gone up and so have the rents. Landlords are eager to get rid of some long-term local residents, since they can charge foreign workers a higher rent.

There are alarming reports of forced adoptions. According to Care Aceh, there are 1,130 documented cases of Acehnese children being taken to Medan, the capital of Sumatra. "The government has done nothing to stop the trafficking in children. It denies that it is happening and then blocks the investigation. The agency in charge is Aceh Sepakat, backed by the government." Some links lead to PKS – a religious party with strong links to the government. According to an eyewitness' testimony, PKS members refused to return a child to a father who recognized (and was immediately recognized by him) his own child, demanding legal documents, which in many cases disappeared during the disaster.

Even at the refugee camp run by the PKS party, the situation is desperate. A member of PKS itself, Mr. Hambani – chief of six Syiah Kuala villages – is obviously frustrated: "You know, I don't even know where their main office is! And I am their member. They gave us almost nothing – some meager load of instant noodles – but when they delivered it, they insisted that we raise their flag over the camp. All they care about is publicity! We got no help from them for 23 days. PKS obviously doesn't care about us, although 80 percent of our community voted for them in the last elections."

INTERNATIONAL HELP

There is no doubt that without the rapid arrival of international help, tens of thousands more Acehnese would have died by now from hunger and disease. As the Indonesian military personnel and police aimlessly hang around the city, military helicopters from dozens of countries are flying to distant and desperate locations of the province, delivering aid, medicine and tents.

Help from the international community is greatly appreciated by the Acehnese people, but makes many officials in Jakarta uneasy. It highlights the inability of the Indonesian authorities to deal with the disaster and allows closer scrutiny of the state and military actions against the civilians and separatists. For a long time, Aceh was off-limits to foreigners. Almost no foreign journalists were allowed in – the official reason being "for their own safety and protection." Now people who have been suffering for years under the military occupation and economic neglect can voice their grievances.

At the same time, Indonesia is counting on international aid to rebuild Aceh. Billions of dollars will be needed for this gigantic undertaking. The question is, how much will get to the victims and how much will go to pay for the latest models of BMWs and luxury villas of corrupt government officials and their business associates from the private sector?

It is no secret that Indonesia is one the most corrupt nations on earth. Graft is institutionalized and touches every sector of society. Distribution of aid is no exception.

Foreign loans can be counter-productive as well. Indonesian international debt as of December 2004 was $78.25 million (with debt service ratio of about 30 percent). The majority of these loans came to Indonesia during the right-wing dictatorship of Suharto. Most of the money never made it to the intended infrastructure, medical facilities and education projects, while the poor and the middle-class (the only ones who are paying taxes anyway) were left with the enormous bill.

Rich countries like the United States and the international financial institutions were well aware of the situation, but continued to suggest new loans. By indebting the nation, they were gaining control over the country and its resources.

Aceh deserves massive foreign aid, but it has to be aid which goes directly to the victims, helping them rebuild their homes and lives, and creates work opportunities. It should not be funneled through the government agencies. Every dollar should be accounted for. If this cannot be achieved, any aid might turn counterproductive!

MILITARY AID AS AID?

After a 13-year break, the U.S. is trying to improve relations with the Indonesian military. Seizing the opportunity that came with the tsunami, it is letting go of its concern around Indonesia's human rights record that led the U.S. Congress to curb military ties in 1992 and cut off Indonesia's eligibility for the International Military Education and Training (IMET) Program and to buy certain kinds of lethal military equipment. After the Indonesian army and its militias rampaged through East Timor in September 1999, killing hundreds of people and destroying much of the territory after the East Timorese voted overwhelmingly in favor of independence from Jakarta, the Clinton administration was forced to cut off all ties.

But the Bush administration has long been eager to normalize military ties with Indonesia – all because Indonesia is seen as a potentially crucial player in the "War on Terrorism," as its army's main concern appears to be to crush the fighters of the Free Aceh Movement.

Since 9/11, the administration has gradually renewed ties by providing aid through new anti-terrorism accounts, resuming joint military exercises, and inviting Indonesian officers to participate in regional military conferences. Condoleezza Rice, the Secretary of State, recently suggested strengthening the American training of Indonesian officers, including training them in modern warfare methods, despite continuing reports of abuses committed by the army in Aceh. In late January, the U.S. supplied Indonesia with $1 million worth of spare parts for its aging fleet of C-130 heavy transport planes that the U.S. sold to Indonesia over 20 years ago. Some say that it is possible that the the ban on the sale of weapons to Indonesia might be removed soon.

Human Rights groups warn that the renewed military aid will be, as in the past, used to suppress independence movements in Papua, Aceh and other hot spots all over the archipelago, and to crush internal opposition and dissent.

The past relationship between the Indonesian government and the United States cannot be ignored. In 1965, the U.S. supported and participated in a military coup which toppled the democratically elected government of Sukarno and imposed the extreme right-wing dictatorship of General Suharto.

Up to 3 million people were slaughtered and Indonesia embarked on the free market experiment which resulted in the social and economic collapse of the fourth most populous nation on earth. While the Clinton administration was forced to break relations with the Indonesian military under immense public pressure, initially the United States and other rich nations (including the UK and Australia) supported the occupation of East Timor which led to a genocide in which one third of the population vanished.

THE FUTURE OF ACEH

Devastated by the military conflict and tsunami, present day Aceh may be one of the most desperate places on earth.

One of the greatest fears of the local people is that after the departure of foreign relief agencies and journalists, it will be hermetically sealed again, left to the mercy of the Indonesian military and government officials in Jakarta.

There is an acute need for a permanent international presence which could monitor human rights abuses and reconstruction efforts. A land-grab of the coastal areas by the government should be prevented and the local people – victims of the tsunami – should be given the choice of whether to rebuild their homes on the present location or to accept relocation.

Human rights agencies should immediately begin a thorough investigation of human rights abuses in the rural areas of the province. There should be decisive support for the referendum on independence. If Jakarta wants to keep Aceh as part of Indonesia, it should offer concessions and perks, instead of keeping the province by force. Above all, the Acehnese people should be the ones to decide their future.

Aceh is rich in natural resources. Suharto and his government signed several deals with multinational companies. For him, these deals brought substantial bribes, but the people of Aceh gained almost nothing. If the Acehnese vote for independence, contracts would have to be renegotiated. This may be one of the main reasons why so far no major foreign power has expressed support for a referendum which would, if held now, almost certainly lead to full independence for Aceh.

If independent, it is still uncertain what path Aceh would choose.

What is certain is that Aceh is injured. It is bleeding, destroyed, confused and tormented by tremendous losses, by uncertainty, and by fear. It is hard to decide where to start solving the complex web of its problems. But the international community needs to intervene now!

February, 2005

Bitter Victory Of Blair

I don't envy my British friends who last week went dutifully to vote for someone they deeply despise. In the UK, people don't vote directly for the Prime Minister; they vote for MPs who in turn pick the PM.

Remembering the reign of three consecutive Tory administrations that turned Britain into an experimental lab supervised by free market fundamentalists, most of the voters thought that they had no choice but to insure that the present status quo, no matter how disagreeable and distasteful, prevails. They felt they simply could not vote for the Conservatives. They closed their eyes and cast their vote for Labor, no matter how "new" and how treacherous it had become. Therefore, Tony Blair, a man associated with shameful lies, survived.

According to Greg Palast: "...The majority of the Queen's subjects – deathly afraid of the return of Margaret Thatcher's vampirical Tory spawn – holds their noses, vote for their local Labour MP and pray that an act of God will save their happy isle. A recent poll showed the British evenly divided: forty percent want Blair to encounter a speeding double-decker bus and forty percent want him to be stretched, scalded and quartered in the Tower of London (within a sampling margin of four percent)."

The "Special relationship" with George Bush and his neocons across the Atlantic is one, but not the only reason, for the scorn so many Britons feel toward their Prime Minister. Blair is obsessed with America, willing to sacrifice social and political principals in his own country which are still dear to so many UK citizens.

The well educated and informed majority of the British public was opposing the invasion of Iraq. However, it was first ignored and then offered a primitive and twisted lecture about democracy and freedom. The lecture was repeatedly delivered in an arrogant tone full of spite, resembling that of an old fashioned secondary school principal.

The British public woke up to a cold reality: no matter how high the percentage of those who were opposing the war, the only voices that seemed to matter were those coming from the White House and Downing Street.

The war was not the only issue surrounded by doublespeak and outright lies. While giving passionate speeches defending the working men and women of Britain, Tony Blair was presiding over the monumental dismantling of what was left of both British Labor and the welfare state. True, he was not alone; the same was happening in Germany which was ruled by the Social Democrats (or should they be called "New" Social Democrats, too?), but he was surely in the vanguard, running closely with his counterpart across the Atlantic.

On the international front, the United Kingdom under Blair, while sounding increasingly compassionate and concerned about the fate of the world's poor (at least two thirds of the planet), remained practically idle and indifferent toward the lands devastated by colonial and more recent neo-colonial policies.

There is no doubt that on almost all important issues, Tony Blair refuses to take into consideration the will of the British people. While he joined the Washington hawks, the British public was demanding peace. While he was assassinating the progressive traditions of Labor, the majority of working men and women felt they didn't ask for it – they were fine with the good old and real thing!

How to defenestrate someone like Mr. Blair from power? Across the rich world, the people of Europe, North America, and Japan are dissatisfied, often disgusted with their rulers, while feeling powerless; unable to find a way to vote into the highest office someone who would represent their interests. They often vote for a "lesser evil" as major political parties look increasingly identical, pushing for almost the same domestic and international agendas.

In the past, voting for Democrats or Republicans in the US, Social Democrats or Christian Democrats in Germany, Labor or Conservatives in the U.K., would make a serious difference and influence the lives of millions of people. Now almost all differences are gone – every major political force is "pro-business," ready to defend the privileges of the handful of countries, companies, and individuals.

Voters are angry and frustrated. Often they choose to "punish" their rulers, applying desperate acts like giving millions of votes to neo-Nazis (Germany and France) – a counter-productive undertaking.

If the political climate was – unscientifically – measured by opinions in the local European cafes and pubs, it would be clear that a majority of Europeans still desire elaborate social safety nets, full employment, free education and medical care, heavily subsidized public transportation – all that is being taken away from them, little by little. Germans (on both sides of the former wall) nostalgically remember privileges of the social state; French and Italians are, in their majority, still closer to 1960s ideals of left-wing parties than to the oligarchic principals of people like Berlusconi.

But people were told – by the media and by the dominant politicians – that the Left was finished after the collapse of the Berlin Wall, that there is no going back. And "a thousand times repeated lie becomes truth." Clichés are not challenged anymore – at least not publicly – as the media became complacent with the system.

The Left didn't die! No matter how often we hear that it did – it is still alive. It was kicked out from the Presidential palaces and PM offices, from television studios and newspapers. But it survived in the hearts and minds of hundreds of millions of voters. They have to make sure that they meet again, find each other – the Left and the citizens. They have plenty in common! For now, Tony Blair will remain in power. But he didn't win. He merely outmaneuvered the British public, employing an antiquated election system which doesn't represent the interest of the people. He is clever enough to know what occurred and one has to wonder whether this victory is going to make him sleep well or feel shame, at least at night, behind closed doors.

In the meantime, the British voters had no choice and they are well aware of it. Paradoxically, unless they demand a change, they may end up – like many in the former colonies where western interests were force-fed through a corrupt political system and through US-subsidized coups – not being able to express their will through the ballot. If they could, they would probably vote for real Labor which is battered but not yet defeated.

May 19, 2005

Colonia Dignidad In Chile - Fall Of The "gods"

The four-lane highway Number Five is smooth and fast, offering outstanding views of The Andes, haciendas surrounded by vineyards and green meadows. It connects the capital with Puerto Montt – more than one thousand kilometers south – and it represents one of the symbols of "the leap forward" Chile has made in the recent years.

Some 350 kilometers from Santiago de Chile, a highway cuts through the humble agricultural town of Parral, a place where one of the greatest poets of the 20th century – Pablo Neruda – was born. One can exit there, then take a narrow picturesque country road straight toward the Andes and to the hot springs of Termas di Catillo.

Sound like an excerpt from a travel guide promoting the endless beauty of the Chilean countryside? Think twice. The shoulders of the bumpy road are now lined with the photographs of men and women who disappeared in this area during the dictatorship (1973-1990). In this area, prisoners were not held in military barracks but in the Fascist German colony named "Colonia Dignidad."

In July 2005, Chilean officials finally discovered caches of machine guns and rocket-launchers, thousands of rusty rifles and endless boxes of ammunition. Interior Minister Jorge Correa declared: "We're talking about a large arsenal and I must stress that it's going to end up being the largest ever found in private hands in the life and history of Chile."

More than 40 years of the outrageous history of Colonia Dignidad is over. What was known for decades to the victims as well as to the inhabitants of this humble part of the country is now in the open: 70 square miles of land owed and controlled by German religious fanatics, extreme right wingers, and child molesters holds some of the most sinister secrets in the history of South America.

In the early 90's, your correspondent spent several months investigating this institution, interviewing dozens of political prisoners from the area, farmers as well as defectors from the colony itself. He was amassing the evidence but there was absolutely no interest in the story: not in Chile, not in Germany, nor anywhere else. The colony had powerful allies, including leading Chilean businessmen and lawyers and top ranking members of the military. Despite the collapse of dictatorship, the colony seemed to be untouchable.

Colonia Dignidad established itself in Chile in 1961. Ironically, its leaders bought the land from a Jewish owner, tricking him into believing that the sect's members were all Second World War victims and refugees. The opposite was true: Paul Schaefer (also known as "Pius" and "Eternal Uncle") – former Luftwaffe medic – was a Nazi who later became a preacher and was wanted by Interpol on the charges of sexual abuse of children in Germany.

Schaefer managed to indoctrinate his followers forcing them to transfer their savings and pension plans to the common financial pool of the sect. After moving to Chile, members were forced to give up all their rights, while laboring in the fields, living in dormitories (men and women separately), and being off from all contact with the surrounding world.

In a relatively short time, Colonia Dignidad became a powerful state inside the state. Surrounded by high-voltage barbed wire and "protected" by the latest surveillance technology and specially trained German Shepard dogs, it became almost entirely self-sufficient. It managed to produce enough food to feed its members and to sell its excess production in the stores of Santiago and elsewhere. It had its own power-plant, airport (big enough to accommodate Hercules transport planes), fleet of cars, buses, trucks and agricultural vehicles; a school, hospital and recording/broadcasting studio.

The official status of the colony was that of a social institution. Doctors were treating (free of charge) local children and adults; school was open to the outsiders from surrounding villages and towns. Only much later was it discovered that while under anesthesia, several patients had their organs removed from their bodies. In exchange for free education, children had to labor in the fields and undergo intensive indoctrination. Leaders of the colony were spreading the word among Chilean villagers that they were visited by the white Gods who arrived in order to save them from their misery.

Sexual abuse of children was widespread. Schaefer and other high ranking members of the colony were entering showers of young boys, selecting victims for sexual abuse. Children had to live separately from their parents. Marriages had to be arranged or at least approved by the leaders. Sexual contacts of unmarried couples were discouraged; those who disobeyed were severely punished. Women who became pregnant "without permission" had two choices: abortion or live in total isolation before the delivery.

Those few members who managed to escape spoke of torture and of chemicals as well as powerful drugs which were given to the members in order to keep them in a constant lethargic state. Letters between Germany and the colony had been censored; radio, newspapers and television sets banned; contact with the surrounding world reduced to a minimum.

Although there is no proof yet, it is widely believed that the colony had hosted on several occasions top Nazi criminals, with the full knowledge of Chilean authorities.

For decades, Chilean immigration policy (as well as that of the neighboring Argentina) was racist. Chile was open almost exclusively to Germans, Austrians, and Czechs – people it believed had high work ethics. Anti-Communist and anti-Semitic to an extreme, the Colony managed to find countless allies in the ranks of local elites.

After the September 11, 1973 military coup (sponsored by the US government and private companies), Colonia Dignidad was converted into a clandestine detention and torture center. According to Ms. Adriana Borquez, one of the victims of torture, members of the colony were using some of the most inhuman practices, which included dogs trained to rape women prisoners as well as tubes with starved rats which were inserted in female genitals.

"Right after the coup, the Chilean military didn't know how to torture," said Adriana Borquez during our long talk in the early 90's. "Prisoners would die very quickly.... Germans in the colony knew how to keep a person alive for several days or weeks while putting him or her through the most terrible agony and humiliation."

It is believed that dozens of political prisoners died on the premises of Colonia Dignidad and are buried somewhere on its territory.

During the dictatorship, ties between the military junta and the leadership of the colony became increasingly close. The Colony's doctor became a personal medic of Pinochet's wife. Schaefer and Pinochet were exchanging expensive gifts, which included Mercedes sedans. Large portions of the funds for the construction of the above mentioned motorway connecting the capital city with the South were channeled through the colony.

The surrounding world paid no attention to what was happening behind the barbed wire of this sinister institution which considered Schmidt and German Social Democrats to be their arch enemies. Proudly spelled out at its entrance: "All that is done here is for Franz Josef Strauss" (referring to the Bavarian right-wing Christian Democratic politician).

In 1985, even the US State Department had to begin its investigation into the disappearance of a US citizen. That year, Boris Weisfeiler, an American mathematics professor – a Russian Jewish immigrant – went hiking in the region. He had been detained by the members of the colony and later executed on Schaefer's orders.

According to The New York Times (May 16, 2005):

> Dr. Weisfeiler's sister Olga visited here last year. "When I asked, I was told that 'we were very young, we don't know, we can't be sure,'" she said in a phone interview from her home in Massachusetts. "So I said to them, 'If you don't know, let's go ask the people who were here and do know.' But they know very well how to do their job, what to answer and how to answer, how to say nothing."

In 1997, Paul Schaefer (officially declared dead for more than a decade) fled Chile. He had been arrested in March, in a suburb of Buenos Aires. Several members of the colony (now still functioning under the name of Villa Baviera) are behind bars, facing prosecution on the charges ranging from torture and murder to the sexual abuse of minors. Continuous raids of Chilean police are finally bringing enough evidence to keep them in prison for the rest of their lives.

However, to see Colonia Dignidad as an isolated case of terror and brutality in Southern Chile would be a mistake. Together with Schaefer and his subordinates, the entire Chilean dictatorship should go on trial. It was not just a "military regime" and "right-wing dictatorship": the period between 1973 and 1990 was nothing less than Fascism in its purest and most explicit form.

July 30, 2005

Hurricane Katrina - View From Asia

More than 8 months ago, one of the worst natural disasters in human history destroyed a substantial part of a province under Indonesian control – Aceh. Although the exact number will never be known, close to 250 thousand people lost their lives during the undersea earthquake and consequent tsunami; tens of thousands died in Sri Lanka, India and Thailand combined. It is now clear that tens of thousands more people died while stranded in remote areas with no food, drinking water, shelter and medical care due to the inadequate response of the Indonesian government and military.

Your correspondent went to Thailand and then to Aceh to cover the extent of the disaster, almost immediately accusing Indonesian authorities of a disorganized, chaotic reaction; of the deployment of religious "volunteers" instead of professionals. He accused the Indonesian military of sabotaging the aid, of stealing food and water desperately needed for those who managed to survive. In one of his reports he concluded that most of the people in Aceh "died because they were poor." Would such a disaster strike in Singapore or in other wealthy nations instead of in Indonesia where tens of millions live in appalling shantytowns, there would be only a fraction of the casualties.

It is now September 2nd, and the cameras of almost all important international news networks are zoomed in on the desperate men, women and children begging for help, abandoned under the brutal sun with almost no food, water and shelter, in one of the greatest historical cities of The United States of America – New Orleans.

Today, one of the reports by Reuters starts with these words: "U.S. troops poured into New Orleans on Friday with shoot-to-kill orders to scare off looting gangs so rescuers can help thousands of people stranded by Hurricane Katrina, find the dead and clean up the carnage." But during the previous days, cameras recorded "looting" by desperate men and women, breaking into the supermarkets and stores, simply trying to survive. Of course there are gangs terrorizing the people in New Orleans area; of course there is shooting and anarchy; but is it the whole story? If the help had arrived sooner, there would obviously have been no need for looting and no chance for gangs to organize.

After flying over New Orleans (no doubt a great sacrifice and expression of solidarity), President Bush spoke about restoring order. It was obvious that defending private property was higher on his mind than the suffering of his fellow citizens. He didn't explain what good is rotting food in partially submerged supermarkets and convenience stores anyway. One wonders whether this is a new and powerful message from his administration: no matter what, private property is untouchable and defending it is of greater importance than saving human lives.

Why did it take US troops so much time to enter New Orleans? Where was all that heavy, high-tech equipment used all over the world, mainly for shameful deeds? On September 1st, the official argument went that an aircraft carrier and several warships had just left the East Coast, and that it would take them some time to reach the Gulf of Mexico. But why didn't they leave earlier, right away, a few hours after the extent of the disaster became known?

Eight months ago the reaction of the Republic of Indonesia was similar: while it takes just a few minutes, at most hours, for its military to blow sky-high known positions of the rebels in Aceh or Papua, after the tsunami, for many days, there was suddenly almost no hardware available for the rescue missions. There were "not enough ships in the area"; soldiers and police on the ground were "too overwhelmed." The government refused to take any decisive action, instead relying on the glorification of the "volunteers."

On the other hand, the Thai Royal Air Force and Navy mobilized almost immediately after the tsunami damaged great parts of its southwest coast. Helicopter crews, some risking their lives, were flying thousands of sorties, trying to save people from the high seas and from affected areas. I encountered several pilots close to the airport of Phuket, late at night, their eyes red from lack of sleep, grabbing something fast to eat before returning to the air – exhausted but determined.

On Thursday, the whole world watched as buses were shuttling people from the Superdome in New Orleans (where almost everything collapsed, from the air conditioning to the toilets) to the Astrodome in Houston, Texas (where thousands of victims of the hurricane were expected to sleep on military beds and share just a few toilets originally designed for the athletes). It was hard to avoid asking: is this really the best the US government can do for those who are experiencing severe trauma, for those who lost everything? This is not Aceh but Houston, Texas, the center of the US oil industry and space program, with hundreds of hotels and motels spread all over the area!

In Thailand, dozens of hotels (and private homes) opened their doors to survivors and to the family members (local and foreign) who were searching for their loved ones. Was it lack of solidarity of corporate America that prevented this from happening in the United States? And if it was, why didn't the government force these hotel doors open for refugees – through an emergency decree? Or is this just another proof that the private sector and private property is sacred, more sacred than human life? Should it be taken as a warning: that from now on things will become this way?

For several days, there were countless images of the Coast Guard helicopters rescuing residents in the flooded areas from their rooftops and from their damaged homes. Helicopters were dropping baskets, pulling victims on board. Most of those rescued did have homes since they lived in the residential areas. At the same time, we were learning that people elsewhere were starving, literally dropping dead in the middle of the streets in the center of New Orleans.

New Orleans is no doubt a segregated city. While it is surrounded by posh neighborhoods (inhabited mainly by whites), the city center and several suburbs are homes to minorities. Some people living there are poor; others very poor. Could it be possible that even during the tragedy rescue operations are treating differently the rich and the poor, black and white? Is there really a lack of helicopters to airlift everyone, to bring them promptly to safety, to give them decent temporary accommodations, private bathrooms and showers?

No matter what the reasons, the response to the tragedy in the Gulf of Mexico was inadequate, scandalously slow; unforgivable. The mightiest military power on earth couldn't (or refused to) deploy soldiers right after the tragedy; it stood by as people were dying in the center of New Orleans which was reachable from the air, at the very least. The government of the United States failed.

Months ago, your correspondent mistakenly claimed that what happened in Aceh could never happen in any developed country. The government that would show such incompetence would be forced to resign. His analyses were proven wrong by recent events in his own country.

In Washington, there are no calls for impeachment and it seems that no heads will roll as a result of this outrageous failure that took the lives of many men, women and children. Criticism in the US corporate press is half-hearted and when it appears, it is diluted by the stories (always so much in demand and on offer) about the heroism and self-sacrifice of the rescue workers. It may appear that although some mistakes were made, society is still governed by sound principles, that in essence everything is correct.

In reality almost nothing went right for the citizens of New Orleans, especially for the poor; and nothing is going right even as these words are being written. White bags are covering the corpses of those who recently died on the streets of New Orleans, those who died after the disaster – long after. Men, women and children are spread on the ground, many almost motionless, in the center of the city. They are hungry and thirsty; they have no place to wash and to urinate. And they are supposed to stay where they are; they are not suppose to "loot" and if they, by any chance, decide to break into some store and take food and water, there are orders to shoot and kill them!

September 01, 2005

Coming Back Home - To New York

New York can be admired or despised, loved or hated, but anyone who has visited this city at least once can't remain indifferent toward it. For some, it is the cultural capital of the world, the most cosmopolitan city on earth, for others a monster growing to the skies, an obnoxious center of global economic power, a place of decadence and indescribable richness; the very symbol of the Empire. Or all the above can be combined.

For many years, New York City was my home. This is where I became an adult man, where I managed to shed my racial prejudices imported from Central Europe; this is where I discovered that the world is round, consisting on hundreds of fascinating cultures, traditions and approaches to life. This is where I scouted countless left-wing and progressive bookstores in the East Village, and learned about jazz in Harlem's Baby Grand. This is where, once a week, I took advantage of the mere six dollar charge standing room area at the very back and very top of the Metropolitan Opera

House. My New York was that of great cheap Indian eateries with live traditional music, of art and revival cinemas, of diverse and intellectually enriching and challenging encounters with people from all over the world.

Even after I physically left the city, it always remained my home, my true center of gravity, my identity.

In the past few years I have lived in many parts of the world: in Central and South America, in Asia and in the South Pacific. An endless desire to discover new frontiers, as well as the depressing political climate in the United States kept me away from New York for more than six years. But the longer I stayed away, the stronger was the suspicion that deep inside I was actually afraid to come back, afraid that there might be almost nothing left of my New York – the city which I knew so intimately; the city that I loved.

Then I had to return suddenly. My film "Terlena – Breaking of a Nation" – about Suharto's brutal dictatorship in Indonesia – was opening in Village East Cinemas. I also had to meet a publisher of one of my nonfiction books. There seemed to be no choice; I booked my flight.

The 18 hour flight from Singapore was endless and exhausting. On board I had plenty of time to wonder what kind of city I would soon encounter: the city that used to be the most open-minded place in the country but which was now electing one right-wing mayor after another; the largest city in the country controlled by obnoxious market-fundamentalists and neo-cons; the economic capital of the rich world that had created seemingly unbridgeable disparities on the planet? Was there anything left of the New York to which I used to belong? Were there still old bookstores, beat-up avant-garde theaters and filthy but magnificent jazz clubs?

My friends wrote to me that New York had changed. The crime rate went down, rents went up and consequently thousands of native New Yorkers couldn't afford to live in Manhattan, anymore. They warned me that New York is now full of chain stores and restaurants, that the uniqueness of the city is rapidly vanishing.

I took a nap on board and my dream (or should I describe it as nightmare) took me to an absolutely unknown New York City: that of flashiness and post-modern steel and glass designs, that of the grandeur and glamor of the only remaining empire on this planet. In that strange dream, almost the entire New York City was enjoying a very high upper middle-class life, prospering from the labor and misery of the third world. It was an indifferent, compassionless, arrogant, overpriced and exclusive metropolis.

I woke up to reality. Singapore Airlines landed at Newark, NJ, surrounded by depressing factories and warehouses. Half an hour later I was being driven for 65 dollars toward Manhattan by an African American cabbie, who indulged in an endless outpour of insults against the present administration. He compared George to several domestic animals and I made myself cozy and comfortable in the backseat, enjoying his colorful monologue more than the ride itself. All he said made sense. I had nothing to add.

Holland Tunnel was clogged with traffic and we took side streets through several dilapidated towns, in order to reach

Lincoln Tunnel. It was the same mess as before; not much had changed. It still looked like home.

The very first evening I was dragged to a party thrown by my friend – a well known concert pianist. A Grand Steinway piano took up half of his living room; it was covered by a thick cloth and being used (for lack of space) as a provisory table for snacks and booze. His girlfriend cooked delicious dishes in something loosely resembling a small-size walk-in closet. It all felt very familiar.

A few days later I went to a new left-wing cable television station operated from a dilapidated downtown loft. I encountered people with well-above-average incomes living in miniscule capsules called "studios." In the meantime I was told that 75 thousand dollars a year before taxes is now a minimum income that can sustain one modest person in Manhattan.

Money seemed to be on everybody's mind. There were well-justified fears of losing mortgages, medical insurance, rent controlled apartment leases. That part seemed familiar, too, but there were also some further developments.

Cheap and fantastic eateries from the past were now few and far between. Almost all Chinese restaurants on the Upper West Side were gone, and so were the Greek diners. Pizzerias had reduced the thickness of the crust. The city was full of overpriced pseudo-Mediterranean trattorias and bistros, and shockingly, there were dozens of brand new junk food restaurants polluting the once fiercely traditional neighborhoods.

Many independent bookstores had closed down, and were replaced by Barnes & Nobles and other book supermarkets. Tower Records and Virgin seemed to be the only places where one could buy music. The galleries of West Broadway had closed down, replaced by Dolce Gabbana and other boutiques. There were almost no "subversive" bookstores in the East Village anymore, but plenty of common shops and eateries instead.

42nd Street had turned irreversibly into a species of G-rated corporate porn. A few blocks away, somebody had come up with the brilliant idea of building a new shopping mall right on Columbus Circle, an obnoxiously tacky and shiny place resembling Manila or Jakarta more than New York City.

I went to the grand re-opening of MoMa (Museum of Modern Art) – that indescribable architectural fiasco hailed by the dominant press as a tremendous triumph – where I learned that from now on, the public would be charged a 20 dollars per person entry fee.

Manhattan used to be like a precise barometer of social problems in this country. Beggars and homeless people were proportionally represented everywhere, living on the same streets as those with seven digit incomes. That was the beauty of New York – nobody could escape reality; everybody was forced to be aware of social problems. Now I noticed a dramatic decrease in the number of beggars on the Manhattan streets. I saw almost no poor people in exclusive neighborhoods. I was told they had been pushed away, swept off like dirt, like garbage. In this sense, New York was turning into a segregated town, not unlike Washington D.C. and Johannesburg.

After visiting "Ground Zero," I decided to take an Uptown E-Train. My friend and I entered the car and the first thing we saw was an old man lying on the floor. His glasses, his instant camera and other belongings were scattered all around him; his wrist was encircled by a plastic band from some hospital.

We found a train conductor and insisted that he immediately call for medical help, which he did, after some hesitation. The train was stuck for fifteen minutes. Then police arrived. They poked into the old man with their clubs: "Hey, buddy! Get up, buddy!" One minute later, three firefighters entered the car. Their presence was truly Kafkaesque. Eventually, the man got up and stumbled out of the car. Paramedics never arrived. "I wouldn't want to have a heart attack in this city," commented my friend.

I'm not mentioning the poor neighborhoods of New York, in this piece. We all know what they look like. I'm not describing true misery. I'm talking about the Upper West Side and Upper East Side, about West Village and So-Ho and other parts of the city that are supposed to be inhabited by the relatively well-off crowd.

After ten days I concluded that most New Yorkers still don't resemble the arrogant victors or self-assured inhabitants of an omnipotent Empire. Most of them look preoccupied and tired, like inhabitants of any large city. They don't appear to be people who are living extravagant, wasteful and lavish lives supported by child-labor in the Philippines or exploited and underpaid Mexican workers on the border. The empire's increasing grip on the rest of the world hasn't made New Yorkers carefree and frivolous; it hasn't given them any extra security. Money from all over the world is pouring through

New York's banks and stock exchanges, but in the end, it rests mostly in the pockets of elites.

Most empires of the past conquered, destroyed and exploited neighboring countries as well as far-away nations. The greatest part of the loot was inevitably grabbed by the rulers, but the rest was usually distributed among common folk. In this respect, the American Empire is unique. The loot stays in a limited number of pockets. The majority of Americans pay for the conquests and foreign expeditions with their taxes, while receiving very little or nothing in return. While the empire is looting, they have to work for their living.

Even if they choose to forget about essential moral issues, New Yorkers and other Americans should ask themselves at least one simple and practical question: "Are we – the citizens of the Empire – really gaining much from the role our country is playing in the world? And if we aren't, then who is?"

January, 2005

ANDRE VLTCHEK grew up in Central Europe and is a naturalized US citizen. Novelist, poet, political novelist, journalist and filmmaker, he has covered dozens of war zones from Bosnia and Peru to Sri Lanka and East Timor. He is the author of a novel *Nalezeny*, published in Czech. *Point of No Return* is his first work of fiction written in English. Other works include the play *Ghosts of Valparaiso*, translated into several languages; and with Rossie Indira, a book of conversations with the foremost Southeast Asian writer Pramoedya Ananta Toer, *Exile*. He writes for several publications worldwide, including *Z Magazine*, *Le Monde Diplomatique* and *Czech Press*. He recently directed the feature length documentary film about the Indonesian massacres in 1965 – *Terlena - Breaking of The Nation*. He presently lives in Southeast Asia.